THE HUMMINGBIRD

Stories, Essays, and Articles
Watching society disappear from the lens

KATHLEENE QUINN

THE HUMMINGBIRD

Originally published in slightly different form in 2017 by Quintessentiale Books, a division of Quintessentiale LLC. Distributed by Ryegrass Press, a Perennial Co.

Where The Light Meets
The Newcomer
In Time and With Water
Dark Tides: The Age of Communication

Library of Congress Cataloging-in-Publication Data

Name: Quinn, Kathleene, author.
Title: The Hummingbird : stories, essays, and articles / Kathleene Quinn.
Description: Second edition. | Seattle, WA : Ryegrass Press / Portfolio, 2020. Identifiers: LCCN 2020915359 | ISBN 978-1-63587-698-7 (hardcover) | ISBN 978-0-463-76485-5 (e-book) Subjects: Psychology—Experimental Psychology | Languages—Communication—Digital Age aspects. | Classification: General Non-Fiction / Literary.
LC record available at www.loc.gov

Printed By:
Ryegrass Press

First Edition: 2017

Printed in the United States of America
10 9 8 7 6 5 4 3 2 1

Contents

Stories, Essays, and Articles

REVIEWS OF WORK

"With subtle simplicity that is almost compelling." – *The Guardian*

"It does not conform to any restrictions of writing which is a breath of fresh air. Almost complicated." – *Publishers Weekly*

"A compelling story about a man whose struggles were rooted from the past and his willingness to get better. This is a personal account with an aim to shed light to the stigma surrounding men's health particularly eating disorder." – *Pulse Magazine*

"An intriguing combination of pigments and pattern, in one of the early works of Kathleene Quinn. Last Winter offers an enigma yet a peaceful approach to soul." – *Paradigm Daily*

For Family and Memories

Dark Tides

THE AGE OF COMMUNICATION

AN ECONOMICS PROFESSOR once said to his class that globalization was a terrible idea. It is a disguised invasion that people of many nations don't realize, however, it might as well be a useful resource mostly for trade benefits. One of the most obvious advantages of globalization is the export market. Production from developed countries can now be sold to other developing countries. It can create employment opportunities and reduce poverty. But underneath the surface more is usually said than done. Major corporations do get an enormous share of profit from the variety of goods made available to other parts of the world. Although it is a worldwide movement, involving integration of financial, communication and economic systems—an uneven proportion of wealth and status elucidate such prevalent marque. There are risks considering with this new environment, taking a closer look into manipulating equality. Conveniently companies from developed countries could outsource jobs to cheaper labor markets than to hire local workers. In the middle of discussion, the professor said something that tickled my curiosity. The concept of *"there's no such thing as a free lunch."* At the end, I gathered the simplest form I could put it into which was, nothing is given for free. For a minute it caught my attention. The man was right. These days you don't get anything for free. You don't do anything for free.

Within two months of working for a new company I was promoted as marketing manager and that was probably one of the highlights of my career. It was very exciting I should say that it lasted for a year before I decided to pursue another path.

First, I had this first impression of selling life insurance to people as stealing. I could've picked a different word, but this was the first thing that came to mind. Let's put it this way, in year 2013 there was an estimated $1 billion of unclaimed life insurance according to sources. The problem being is the lack of communication between the insurance companies and policy holders. When an insurance company is left uninformed regarding the passing of a person the policy will eventually be delinquent or discontinued. This can be very difficult for the family as well. Another problem is that most beneficiaries are unaware of such insurance policy. In 2016, the numbers have gone up to $7.4 billion, of which $5 billion will hopefully be distributed to the beneficiaries found in the data. However, we all know that insurance is important. A healthcare insurance particularly is like an admission ticket to hospital.

I received an email from an old client asking if I would be interested in doing a little project with his team. During that time, the cunning business of search engine optimization has slowly crawled up into the radar of many companies. They figured out a way to leverage their presence in digital marketing. Now mind you that not all businesses were well equipped when it came to this. Even now. They had no idea what content marketing was about, so they ended up hiring people who could do the work for them. Mark's team in Salt Lake has been doing it for a while, they were basically contracted by other businesses for these types of jobs. I was just lucky enough to get on the ride and see how everything goes into play.

Having different kinds of jobs was an advantage for me, I was able to apply them in so many different areas. I didn't have that much of an experience to any of the jobs, but I did them anyway. Even if I failed, I would still have learned something from it.

It is not about passion or hard work. It is about ambition. It is about self-awareness. When you have a clear vision of what you want to accomplish in life, you will do all the good things possible to get there. Although some may take it farther. It is not just about passion otherwise you would do things for free—you love it so much you will do it anyway. There's no guarantee. You must take a leap. When you are ambitious enough to reach your goals in life you can do great things. Although there is danger in ambition. You are your own enemy. The realization you make will guide you to a path that you've always wanted to go.

One of the greatest works of literature called Great Expectations is a metaphor to ambition and transformation. Nobody said it was going to be easy. But how bad do you want it? That is the question. When Pip realized that he was in love with Estella he was shooting for the moon. He knew he needed to change his life to be worthy of her. It was his motivation to changing himself. Although it was made possible by his mysterious benefactor. For a moment he knew what he wanted. He didn't want to go back to his old life—of being a poor orphan living in the countryside. That he must surround himself with powerful rich people and those who were in position. He would learn and soon become one of them. A gentleman. One can imagine how extremely difficult that was for him especially during a time wherein wealth and social class define oneself. When he went to London he didn't know what to expect. He was sent to get his education—where a much better life awaited for him. A different one. At first, he was self-conscious and inferior to all things that were new. His etiquette was, of course, tested as he mingled around with other people. Everyday he was slowly adapting to his environment—the only way he could survive as well as play the game. The main character Pip, needed that one motivation for him to get started. It seemed like his ambition has awaken him along with his affection for Estella. A coming of age story however delivers the metaphor anyone could use to contemplate on what matters in life.

Sometimes a realization doesn't come in an instant. A lot of people are wandering without knowing what they truly want. What makes them happy? What is their purpose? What matters? These are some of the questions being asked. And because life is a journey itself each of us will continuously learn and grow. Supposedly.

INFLUENCE AND VALUE

"The key is to keep company only with people who uplift you, whose presence calls forth your best." – Epictetus

You are as good as the company you keep. Who is the greatest influence in your life right now? It is rather relevant to where you intend to go. When I was in college, I thought I wanted to be a lawyer or an architect. Just like anyone who was given the idea of paid occupation. I ended up working in a different company. I lost contact with my college friends. Getting an offer the same day I had my interview was a big deal for me. Although that company was on my top five list, I wasn't really sure what to expect. But I remember the manager who did my final interview. I envied her communication skills. She talked with such poised and precision. She explained the core values of the company, vision and mission, all that stuff. So I thought, I want to work in human resources and eventually be in the same position like her. Of course, that didn't happen. I was hired as a customer relations specialist. That time I was just happy to get a job. I didn't feel the need to fill my thirst for creativity until the day I realized it's time. There were two call scenarios I claimed to have given me the hint or sort. First, an old man who cursed the hell out of me. He was madly upset with the bill he just received and called out the company for being a cheat. Having a terrible and incompetent service, he threatened that he would sue the company. He also demanded for a compensation for all the inconvenience this had caused him. He was a retired accountant and quite frankly I didn't feel qualified enough to argue with him in that case. Or simply I didn't feel like it. I was shaking and at a loss for words. I knew

I had to pass that call to my supervisor. Second, a widow. A very nice old lady who was calm and gracious during the entire conversation. She asked about me and my interests. It was an easy call because she was moving and so I needed to update her billing address to where all her billing statements would go. And then she asked me if I was happy with what I do. I gave myself a pause. I asked myself the same question in my head. I knew the answer. Then I told her *Yes*. That was the end of the call. I didn't bother to further my answer because of time constraint. Also, I was thinking that our quality assurance leader might be listening on the other line. But in that moment I felt a sudden rush. As if something pinched me in the arm. My answer was the opposite. When I figured that out I knew I had to move on. That's when I got my next job. I continue to learn everyday. It was like putting eggs into my basket. I just knew that if I work in that field I will eventually crack a code that would allow me to pursue my true passion. I had to be surrounded with that kind of people because they fueled my level of energy and enthusiasm. It was a different challenge for our team that had sole responsibility of pleasing a client. You should know establishing a brand is not an easy task. When you are introducing a product to an audience nonetheless the market, it is walk on a thread. A key ingredient is very important. People are curious. They are looking for something different about it. When you understand people, you understand business. It was a matter of time that I hit a spot, I talked to our account manager and asked for a raise. I knew I had so much to put on the table. I was confident enough with the kind of value I bring to the company. A week passed after that meeting and it felt a little awkward. My teammates who probably heard the news acted different toward me. I really didn't care. I was only concerned with one thing. Promotion.

As you grow with the company you will find yourself searching for fulfillment. You maybe happy with your latest accomplishments but the difference lies on the validation of your title. It is important that you give value to what you do. Learn its worth. Yes, they want loyalty. They want retention. If you are the best of what you do, you get to stay. You will step up. Have a thick skin because you will need that in the game. When it comes to influence, we only have good or bad. We were taught of that in the early days. Choose your people. Choose the company that you keep. Because you are the average of the five people you hang around with. There's no emotional attachment. Making friends is good. Having friends is wonderful. The ones who will stick around. Those who will have your back and lift you up when you are down. The ones you can count on. The true ones. Yes, don't waste your time. Explore and expand. Allow yourself to learn. Surround yourself with the good kind of people. If you want to grow; if you want to improve. You must connect. You have to ask for help—from the ones who have been there and done that. This is not to discourage but rather to encourage you. Build and network. That's just how it works. Even now when you see a competition you would want to be in a winning team. In reality, people like to win. We aspire to be successful. We dream of greatness.

We know that influence is very important in business but so is value. Know what type of value you bring to the company. What type of value your product has to offer? What makes a great product? It's not just about the material as much as functionality. A great product is solution to problem. It is an entity that supplies the needs of the consumer. It should be flexible, durable, and useful in so many ways. It should not be a costly item either, but it is something that every person would want to buy.

Undoubtedly iPhone has cemented its name as far as mobility and interface will go. It truly has changed the perception of communication and data. It has made an impact to people to make things a lot easier with a touch of your hand. When Steve Jobs first introduced iPhone in June 2007 some people thought it was a bad idea. While competitors were on their seats waiting to get a glimpse of what was deemed impractical and over-priced product, the world had witnessed a leap of technology. It was a question if people would've actually bought a phone with no keyboard or stylus, which were the characteristics of PDA and smartphones back in the day. However, days before its released people were already lining up in front of Apple stores in tents as if there was a reunion concert or audition for American Idol.

People were excited and curious about this iPhone. Of course, that wasn't the first time Apple has brought the crowd frenzy. When they released iPod the music industry glazed its way to a new level of interconnection to which people will enjoy thousands of songs compressed in a single gadget. People were willing to pay for such item. A thousand songs in your pocket for $399 seemed worth it that time. As for iPhone it was easy to convince the public starting at $499 for 4GB of memory. But then again this was the phone that changed the world. If you want to be a part of that guess you have to pay the price. For many startups and entrepreneurs per se giving a price tag to a product is not easy. Although being expensive is often mistaken for a good quality. These days it's not necessarily true. In fact, the justification of a product should not be based on price, at least not alone. The difference between $100 versus $1,000 suit is the sale.

Wires of Engagement

When you learn to establish yourself before the brand then you are likely to get their attention. That means don't try to sell anything at first meeting. It has been one of the misconceptions these days. Ask yourself, how you would feel when you get a random email about a magazine subscription, perhaps a relatively new publication that you haven't heard of. More likely you wouldn't pay attention to it and will keep scrolling down or will hit the delete button as it is something that doesn't interest you. All the more if it was asking you to subscribe.

The market is unpredictable it's shifting by the moment. This can't be blamed to technology. It is human behavior. Time has changed. The definition of necessity is not only limited to what encompasses the basics. These days more people are living a lifestyle they can't afford or don't need. When this happens the chance of a price to go up is inevitable. It is how supply and demand works. When the seller figures out the consumers are willing to pay as much, he will think he can get more money for whatever is being sold. But that's business right. You can expect a ridiculously overpriced item, if you get it from an upscale store. People are continuously and unknowingly supporting these types of products. Again, don't blame the economy nor technology, but human behavior. There's something about spending that pushes the value. As long as people are patronizing a certain product—it will continue to exist in the market. I have no problem with spending, but I only spend my money on something that makes sense.

When it comes to competition, there is a saying that goes—*"if you can't beat them, join them."* While the market is tough you have to be tougher. Getting into this ruthless business needs more than just talent and hard work. It also needs persistence. Try and try and try. In one of Denzel Washington's speeches he said that if you hang around in a barber shop long enough, you'll soon get a haircut. And that's true, you hang around with the right people you are going to learn something from them one way or another. But here's the thing, patience and persistence are crucial in any field. You must prepare yourself for whatever is going to happen. In business, there will always be competition. So how about this—dominate and not compete.

"The key of persistence will open up any door that has been closed by resistance." – John Di Lemme

There's a reason why you are doing what you are doing. And regardless of that reason—that is an element of motivation that gets you going. Knowing what you want gives you an advantage in life. You may not realize but it makes a difference when you have a vision. Aside of course from making profit— good intention is apropos to giving value. If you are looking for a long-term plan whether in business or career— connection and establishing relationship will do good simply because of the value that both parties offer. Scratch my back and I'll scratch yours, right. Be likeable, be consistent. If you are a team player, you are most likely to get a badge. But you are also sending them an impression of you being reliable.

Whether you like it or not there is a price to pay for whatever it is you are asking in life right now. But with ambition, persistence and good intention things will fall into place. When that day comes you will feel that sense of fulfillment.

People feel entitled of certain things. You might think life owes you something but that's not the case. We either do something or not. We maybe existing but that doesn't mean living. A young man named Roger worked in a bank for six months. That was his first job after he finished college. He decided to quit because he thought he wasn't making an impact. He was tired of his daily routine cashing checks. He was not happy. Like him, there are many Rogers in the world today. Those people who are unhappy with their jobs. They simply show up to work for the heck of it and to get a check. But that's about it, there's no meaning or purpose. As if there's a void that needs to be filled. The consciousness is somehow yelling to do something about it. Now each person has his own dilemma. Although this does not constitute an ending as soon as they realized there are other resources. If you think like a leader it would be difficult for you to follow such guidelines. You see yourself far ahead that you don't want to be a part of the pack, instead you want to lead the pack. And leaders do think differently. But for a leader to be successful he or she needs to understand process. They need to understand people. When he puts himself before his people, he disregards the opportunity to make an impact. This is how companies thrive. They set forth goals with their people. And for some of them, they see their value when they are tasked to be a part of something bigger. I feel valuable when I know I am needed, that fraction of my work is part of the structure that helps the company stand on the ground. Doing what you are supposed to is necessary, understand that work is fundamental to everything that you do. Everybody needs to take that first step. The sense of fulfillment is found when you give yourself the chance to learn.

The mind is wired for convenience and connectivity. We are used to things that are within reach. We have great expectations in life. When things don't go our way, we feel discouraged and uninspired. This factors on what hinders a man's true potential. The fear of failure. Some people don't see the prize they only see obstacles. The only way to get to your destination is when you keep moving. In times of uncertainty your patience and determination will be tested. This time you will be reminded of the resources you have that don't limit to tangible ones. Individual resources gained from previous experiences are useful in the matter of real-life situation. Applying what you have learned from the past is compelling in problem solving and decision-making scenarios.

The Hummingbird

The company I worked for was one of the leading solutions company. It was up and coming but able to pull the biggest account which was Dell. It served small and large businesses from web development, social media marketing, conversation rate optimization and so on. It was recognized by Inc. 500 and featured in many different media outlets. In early 2000, search engine optimization emerged to be one of the most powerful tools to manipulate traffic for businesses that wanted to increase their presence in the worldwide web, while its existence can be traced around the 1990s. It was considered as a marketing discipline in growing audience. It was perceived as trick of the trade in driving customers to a profile or organization. It isn't a platform but a service that functions to give name to what was once unknown. To create a buzz if you will. But it was also the type of service that fed ideas to people of which encompassed information whether it was true or not. For the most part I thought about it as subjective role to guiding people in finding whatever they were looking for. I enjoyed that job and learned a lot from it. Today it still is an outlet for visibility in search engine results. As true and ironic as it is that tv commercials are crippled by the existence of Facebook, Twitter, and Instagram—these giants are thriving because of advertisement itself.

In fact, consulting industry is making a lot of money. Most of the businesses today don't know where to start in building their online presence, because that's how it works now. If you have a pastry shop you would want your customers to be able to find your website. At least, some business owners are aware of that. Gone are the days that you pay a local newspaper for an advertisement. Although many of you will say everyone has Facebook account. I would like to think that social media should be a choice for every person. Yes, it is revolutionary for some of the greatest minds and interesting topics are being shared in a click of a button. It's fast, thrilling, controversial. Then there is cyber bullying. A terminology they have coined for the sake of internet reference. This issue, however, has gone way beyond out of control. According to cyber bullying statistics from the iSAFE foundation, over 25 percent of adolescents and teens have been bullied repeatedly through their cellphones and the internet. The Hartford County Examiner also reported that only 1 in 10 teenagers will tell a parent if they have been a victim of bullying on the internet. This all entailed postings of embarrassing or damaging pictures without their permission. A problem that needs immediate action, as it has escalated to suicide cases. Someone said that people have given up their privacy long ago when they created profiles on dating websites. Being cautious is simply not enough when you have already stored your credit card details to purchase a purse from an online store. It is true there is good and evil on the internet. Mankind has managed to create one of the most treacherous tools of all time. Social media has its way of bearing both the positive and negative. The way we utilize it is an aspect that needs more than just prohibition of the unacceptable. It needs thorough assessment of setting standards not only to people but to the platform itself—as the provider has its shared responsibilities when it comes to the cause and effect of the channel.

Dirt and Dusk

There are two types of audiences based on traffic—organic and inorganic. In marketing it is important to penetrate to different channels that would allow you to gain these audiences who are likely to become consumers. In other words, an audience doesn't necessarily mean paying customers. It is a general public looking for products. They are passive, however, doesn't rule out the possibility of becoming real customers. For now, they are observers.

As viscous as it may sound we know that popularity metrics are based on likes and views. As if it is a chemical reaction to a person's mind and body to be able to get as many likes as possible—it somehow releases stimulant. The whole thing excites us when we see that our post is appreciated by the people. The form of communication has totally drifted to a different level. Everybody feels the need to get connected. It is already hard to keep up with the millennials, especially not when they feel entitled to conveniences in life. According to The Center for Generational Kinetics, millennials are those who were born between 1977 and 1995, while others would say that it was from 1982 to 2002. Although you'd probably still hear some who would complain from time to time but think about the accessibility and resources there are now compared to when we had to scour encyclopedia to find the answers. The deep challenge of transcending messages from one end to another wherein they are not filtered or saturated by media is evident. Everything happens so fast.

Communication and its definition is subdivided to its context. The exchange of information appears in several categories. But let's take social communication for instance, how it is defined in the society these days. What does it mean to communicate? How do we communicate? When we look at the simplest definition of this—there's social communication that refers to language that is used in social situation. The main point of interacting with others and being in a group that discusses ideas and topics. This what makes social media communication intriguing. Everyday you see something different, something familiar. But it evokes comments and feedback. The purpose of posting articles in blogs and photos on Instagram is not only limited for reading or viewing. It is to knock into our consciousness of what is happening. What is current? Every individual is entitled to his opinion they say. You see that everyday when you read comments that are both positive and negative. The deconstructive idea brings forth a challenge in form of critical review to a person, place, thing, or event. Some might take it personally but others see it differently. When the truth is presented in front of you it does hurt. But it is necessary in order for us to grow. Not unless if you rather live in pretend.

When we are compelled to speak our mind and discuss them with another person we don't necessarily have to ask them a question. It would be nice to start off by asking how the person is doing. "*How are you?*" is the most common greeting that is understood by most languages in the world. It is simple but valuable to show grace and manners to one another. A conversation is like an organ to communication. A part of its core if that makes sense. A good conversation is not only good to establish rapport in making connections with other people but scientifically healthy in terms of brain activity. In a research study by Princeton University, they found that when good conversation is established it would initiate the linking of the brain that is part of the process when there is speaker and listener. The term "coupling" is when more regions are active extending into brain areas that involved higher thinking such as the process of meaning of language.

The expansion of social media communication is taking communication into different forms. As the platform is not only limited to posts and articles. It has its own section for sending private messages and although depending on the channel the characters might be limited, the contact is initiated. The idea of "freedom of speech" and its interpretation—is misleading. Feeling entitled to your own opinion doesn't mean you can say whatever you want to say. And for a long time, people still don't get it. There are things that are better left unsaid.

Although "*pay secrecy*" in workplaces is no longer abided in most cases. The National Labor Relations Act has long held the policy as violation to the law. Even if the employee signed a nondisclosure agreement with the employer, he or she would still be protected when talking about salary. But exchanges in communication that might compromise the information of the company including its clients is a different scenario. Status or the current state of being is not only limited to events but also to one's opinion. You see people everyday feeling grateful and optimistic while others are grumbling and boastful. There are so many ways this could go but it shows us how a channel is being used one way or another.

In media and politics there is only information and criticism. That nature is typical and predictable. News reporters and staff utilize social media as an extension to what has been broadcasted. It serves as an emphasis or a follow up to the latest discussion. Not all stories are news. And news is not but a story if without an audience. The way I see it based on the headline.

Imagine if you didn't have to go anywhere or idly sitting at home, you'd probably spend more time in social media rather than watching the television. Not to disregard the shows to-binge-watch on Netflix. But people are easily drawn to what's within reach. The phone is more powerful than ever. It has continued to evolve and function not only for the sole purpose of communicating with others but as streaming device that is source of data. Everything that is happening in the world is on the web and as long as we have access to it, we are able to follow. The way communication has expanded its form gives an impact to what serves its purpose.

But today it is not enough to have a social media account in order to establish a brand, connect to people or simply spread the news. The factor being is—competition. With that said you are in competition to people's attention. When everything is in front of us. We have the power to choose. With all the mediums there are. Content is a valuable trade that makes your brand worthy of attention.

"Mountaintops inspire leaders but valleys mature them."
— Winston Churchill

Engaging with people is a skill you must learn for them to stick around. You can't just ask anyone to like or follow your brand without showing them "*why*" in the first place. Your contribution in the field is prerequisite to what adds value in what you do. People want your product not because of how you do it but because of why you are doing it. So going back to the question, how often you should spend time in using social media. There is no definite answer. It is a variable as long as it continues to float. Think about it as your vehicle—it moves as long as somebody's driving it. I wouldn't tell you to spend your entire day following and messaging people and liking their posts in the hope of getting their attention. And maybe you'll do but there are far better things to do out there.

That is why I consider social media as an artifact. An item of culture. Although it is present and not buried in history, it is an intangible tool that is part of us.

One day all of these things won't even matter but whilst we have them we might as well grasp the moment. But use it wisely. Connect with others. Express your passion. Don't limit the goods of technology to what it already is. Go beyond the boundaries of what is needed. What can be done? There's more to this medium than making profit. If we are going to make it a habit, let's make them good and put it to good use. I believe in utility and function. I believe in material. But I also believe a single action will have its ripple effect which maybe good or bad. However, when using the tools that we have now we must consider the consequences later.

The Culture That Is

As time changed so did the people. We have learned to adjust in our own environment perhaps with a little knowledge that whether we like it or not we have to live or at least try to follow the norms that are expected from us in the society not necessarily conforming but adapting to its changes. Although it varies from one culture to another there are certain things that serve as common denominator to us. Communication is one good example. Regardless of the difference in language, we attempt to connect to one another and by that we use available tools to bridge the gap. In political interests it serves as an accelerator for movements with mass appeal. With social media you will gain followers not only for your business but for greater cause. The community has learned to embrace its nature and with the relentless aspect of technology. It has become easier to target people or a group that is suited for the benefit or purpose.

It is showing us different ways the tools of communication can be of used. Whether it's written or audio—the messages are encrypted into these formats for us to unscramble and understand. Even without translation we feel the urge of understanding the message for the most part because we are curious. We are searching for answers. But part of coexisting is communicating—and because it has been misread and misinterpreted at most times there is chaos. It is quite interesting when most blog sites are doing culture pieces as content to start an engagement. Where food and travel reviews are actually getting more responses from the audience. In fast paced environment people are actually searching for something outside the reality. The busy life is keeping them from doing the other things that interest them. But traveling is one thing that everyone wants to do at some point if given the chance. We all want to go and visit some places and the ones we haven't been before.

Videos are not only showcasing the landscape imagery of the different destinations but also to build connection to people in different parts of the world. I remember watching the GoPro HERO3 ad some years ago which has now 44 million views on YouTube. It still gives me the goosebumps. A different feeling of seeing through the beauty and wonders of life in a compact digital device.

Make a Mark

How do we remember a brand? What makes a brand stand out? With all the major brands taking a leap in the online market era, its biggest competition is not the other brands but the space itself. Of what has become the open field for everyone who can create websites, the new and upcoming businesses of this time are somewhat taking over the direction of what it means to be a brand.

It raises the question, to me, if they are aware that being a brand is more than just selling hats and t-shirts. Better yet it is more than just selling any physical products. It is making a statement, a representation of a cause. When Steve Jobs founded Apple, he wasn't thinking of a business in itself. He thought of a company that came with a purpose. At that time, they wanted to create a company that has a lot to do with learning particularly in higher education. Those that involved software that can be used in college and university campuses. Admittedly that was thinking big. That was a vision. And so today if you think of these seemingly systematic individuals or groups who have created different products uprooted from the idealist stereotype of passive income, it makes you wonder what type of value they bring to the market.

Workplace

LinkedIn which has a revenue of $2 to $5 billion (USD) per year has sustained its spot amongst other tech companies when it comes to friendly work environment. Their CEO Jeff Weiner has emerged as the Highest Rated CEO of 2017 according to Glassdoor. As there were many factors considered in the result based on research and company reviews one key element that is important to most employees when it comes to work satisfaction and professional growth is leadership. A lot of times this is overlooked in some companies and nowadays a debate of what it takes to be a good leader. There are people who actually enjoy working with others and feeling fulfilled by the tasks assigned to them. The sense of belonging fuels them go on everyday—not just a mandatory state of being but happy and content with their jobs. Imagine yourself working in one of the biggest companies in the world where creativity and ideas are encouraged and celebrated instead of being repressed and controlled. Where your hard work is appreciated and rewarded. This is the kind of a place you would want to be. Aside from the benefits and incentives employees do like to work in safe, fun, and positive environment. This is why big dogs like Google, Facebook, LinkedIn, and others have redesigned the traditional look of an office space. They discovered that employees and performance are impacted by work environment. So turning tables around where accessibility and flexibility are no longer restricted. The companies of today are becoming more aware of their to do's when it comes to improving their space. Not that physical environment is the only thing that matters as to attract employees but other things like: employment equality, diversity, career growth and work friendliness.

Today companies should aim for retention of employees. Where they are the frontliners they should be given enough attention to what makes them happy as well as stay in the company. The company I used to work for had around 186 employees in the building, however, managed to arrange meetings in fashionable order where they could listen to their people. That was very important in a way of establishing continuity and progress. When a company gets to keep their employees especially the good ones, they have the advantage of moving forward and fast. While others are not paying so much attention to their recruitment, they are also losing time and money. This being when they have to go back on training new employees which could be long-drawn-out. So, if it's less than of a hassle to talk and listen to them better do it now. If communication is your capital—establishing good relationship in the company makes it more fun to work at.

The Captain

Being a leader is not just about making good or bad decisions. It is not about implementing rules for the people and company. It is not about having clear vision of the goals you set for the company. It is not just knowing where to go, but knowing where to take the people where you want to go.

"The function of leadership is to produce more leaders, not more followers." — Ralph Nader

Leadership is a skill. The simplest way of saying it, and it is. When one soon realizes to put himself last, and think of the people he is responsible for. A good leader is unselfish. He is willing to make sacrifices for his people. It doesn't matter if there are ten, hundreds, or a thousand employees, he will make the best choice for the benefit of the many. One can easily say "I am a leader" but in reality it is an anointment of whether you have the trait and heart of carrying the people in every step. Most successful companies reach their destination not because of one person alone but that they worked together as a team. A holistic embodiment of togetherness and cooperation. The unique perspective of knowing and taking care of the people is an essential element. More than just being a role model and communicator to every individual but also the capacity to bring forth an organization and what it stands for.

Beyond the Walls

A great deal for me when it comes to technology and online media is the potential of breaking barriers. For those who were not favored to attend college or witness a great lecture from a reputable university creating an open course made available for anyone in the world who has access to internet is an opportunity for learning at its best. In the second year of my graduate studies I have found myself searching for answers about the different practices in the field of Public Health. With that said, young generation poses threat to undermine the value of education viewing it as burden instead of opportunity. That one doesn't need it to be successful in life and not a requirement whatsoever. While you may not need a PhD in order to get a decent job, you will definitely need your education to get ahead. An intimidation to culture when most people consider a life of business instead of work, a neglect of education to be a nomad of his own land. Arguably the skills mismatch is present in the workforce today. The way to excuse unemployment by filling out positions with people of different qualifications. Everyone is entitled to great education and this should be taken into advantage. However, with the presence of online education, there have been less interaction between the students and teacher. Email serves as communication tool on this platform. While some classes require participation by posting comments and answers in their forum. This type of function will allow students to take their time in finding answers however taking away the essence of extemporaneous learning. The outright benefit of having been surrounded with other peers, will carry out to one's behavior. The social skills acquired at an early age can be a factor to self-confidence and independence.

Words that Count

There is a question of whether the written expression is influenced heavily with the symbols and emojis normally nonequivalent to the traditional alphabet. The predicament of practicality to adjustment. A need to draw lines between the tendencies of speech errors coming from native and non-native English speakers in relation to articulation disorder. The factors will have to be considered when diagnosing a person with speech error such as cross-linguistic influences, early language acquisition for L2 and prosodic tendencies. In 1994, Taylor & Payne suggested that accents are sound differences of a spoken language and are usually attributed to geographic regions and influences of foreign languages. The disfluency transfer in reading and speaking may well inhibit the diagnosis in terms of articulation disorder while taking some factors into consideration. This is important rather than pre-judging mispronunciation and background.

There are several theories about how language works in our minds, in an attempt to understand its components, relatively associating meaning and sounds—using syntax, that is, putting words in order to come up with a thought, understanding strings of words called sentences. In 1960, theories represented by the mentalist Jean Piaget and the empiricist Rudolf Carnap were ones of the most established. The linking between linguistics and psychology in studying a child's development toward language—early stage development while putting explanation into behavior response.

As per cognition the words will come out from our mouth naturally as they are being processed inside our head (Broca's area). The spoken words will coincide a situation, emotion, and intention. However, a speaker is responsible for the utterance. Chomsky and others, such as Lenneberg, in 1967 noted the universality of language. They pointed out that language is learned by people of all cultures, in all environments, and in very similar stages. Although they are different in some levels the common denominator there is, that being a tool for communication. There is also a noted difference when it comes to accent, dialect and intonation coming from a specific group in the society. For example, those who speak English as a second language are known to have more grammatical and speech errors. However, it does not necessarily suggest of them having communication problem since they are normally fluent in their own dialect. There are regions with softer vowel sounds, thus, the transfer of pronunciation when it comes to English being the second language flow easily. We also have to consider that without the available knowledge in language acquisition especially during their early stage, factors of being non-fluent in English is still a question. The acquisition of a second language depends on the ability of the speaker to adapt into a new set of rules in the realm of linguistic principles and attributes.

Communication barrier decreases self-esteem while limiting social interaction. Since language is a matter of cultural difference, we must examine its roots. Language itself is a variable at this stage. The learning of language as a child counts as the first step and foundation of his native tongue. Language is common but different at the same time.

When dissecting the components of each word that makes up a statement, we understand the meaning. Although they can be independent, their places and functions are suggested. Thus, when a speech error occurs it will somehow rearrange the thought behind each linguistic element. There are also speech errors which only occur in constant cases in terms of phonemes.

In this case cultural aspect is still being considered yet unless the speech error is coming from an English native speaker. A study by the Department of Linguistics in Northwestern University showed that occurrence of speech errors is spontaneous.

In psycholinguistics—they have studied a child's ability to learn a language in a way of experimental or quantitative methods, which was different from the naturalistic observations of Jean Piaget. In which he also suggested the developmental stage of language acquisition.

A language is not nurtured without a speaker who exercises it. The existence as well as evolution of language also depends on its ongoing usage within a society. A speaker will have to use certain language in order to communicate. There is also a degree to which a speaker may have used such words when expressing anger, excitement, happiness, disappointment, etc. Sometimes a speaker will have to use hand gestures emphasizing certain words and giving more weight to the expression.

A language only exists when it is being used by a group of people in the society. Our culture plays a vital role for its existence. One can also notice the uniqueness and diversity of a language that makes it interesting. While others believed that learning a different language is a way of relating to people.

There are several theories on how language works in the human brains, in an attempt to understand its components, relatively associating meaning and sounds.

An interesting theory called the Speech Act has been a long-term debate in the field of Linguistics. The challenge of breaking down the true meaning of a person's action. In 1962, John L. Austin originally published a book called "How To Do Things With Words" which was a huge success. He believed in the development of performative utterances. It is the act of doing something by saying something. For example, you ordered coffee then most likely you will get a coffee.

The role of social media is to disseminate information. A lot of times this is being overlooked. We don't underestimate social media in terms of it being a product or tool of communication—it is not only a result of technology but rather a component of cultural shift. Technology is part of our existence. It is a revolution. And by itself the categories that come underneath are also moving swiftly toward a new era. People should be more sensitive when it comes to utilizing their tools and power. And by power I meant authority. You might have the advantages of today but what about tomorrow. The only path to go is where everybody's attention is going. But just like the stock market it goes up and down. Yes, work is important. Nothing is given in this world. Nothing. Successful people have sought the importance of adjusting to the changes in the environment. When retail businesses started to slow down in early 2005 with the emergence of ecommerce many have tried to dodge the reality that it was becoming more than just a trend. Of course, some have already seen it coming even before Facebook Ads, Shopify, and YouTube. All these tech giants are dominating the cyberspace industry by adding value to what was already a demand.

The sensibility of media these days are thrown off a lot with all the perplexities in both sides. People who care enough to watch the news and want to know what's going on in the society are curious at the same time knowledgeable. It gives more advantage to anyone who does not pay attention to the current events. Information is within reach not only limited online. Print media is still hanging on and will likely last for a while. Although the decline in newspapers and magazines has totally changed the game of publishing. However, it didn't cease the entire industry. Unknowingly there's a whole different niche that is created through the digital platform bringing audience to a new type of communication. As advertisers are willing to pour millions of dollars to put their brands on the leading platforms, there have been a rise of content marketing. Brands are collaborating with other brands as a new technique of guiding consumers to products. This is not a surprise as both parties could get the desired benefit. When blogging started it was more like a diary of a person's daily activities. But later transitioned to be a tool for marketing and promotion. In some ways, a portfolio of the favorites and experiences while showcasing consumed products. That moment triggered many companies a possibility of combining critical opinion and customer experience as to lure other and future customers. But it was not that easy at first. And nothing is. It has to be a process. And with the demand of all these types of bloggers who can present themselves as experts in creating content for clients whether it be in fashion, technology, hotel, restaurant and travel, the space could only get bigger and bigger. It also means competition. When Facebook first started, nobody predicted it to be an essential tool for business. Like a very important one. In one of Mark Zuckerberg's interviews, he had no idea he was building a business more so an empire that would change the way of social communication. The case of communication spread out through these different channels is astonishing. With a simple click of an article post one can amplify a single topic that resounds into the community. We share the same information without knowing we are influenced.

The thing about success is not something you can pass around. It's not tangible you see. But the components that made an individual successful can be taught as shared knowledge. Utilizing resources in the right way will eventually pay off. Let us not ignore the tools of communication and that they should be used the right way. Now, we are passed pen and paper. We chat down notes on our phone—the single device an individual must have in today's time. So many of those high school and college students are learning the basics and even more technical skills in video editing just as when they're making videos for YouTube. What they did next was an important aspect in life that everyone could learn from. It's the action. For every passion there can only be an action. If it's that important to you. If that's what you want to do. Then do something about it. I didn't imagine myself working for a newspaper right after I graduated from college. It was more of a vague career choice because I had not made up my mind at that time—not knowing what I really wanted to become after I got my degree. I believe a lot of you have experienced this dilemma before. Even if you are an A student there is no guarantee that success will be handed to you. You still have to work hard for it.

Ironically despite the technological advantages of today, we still fail to get our message across. How to make sure our information is used accordingly? I say this amidst all the issues and scandals that everyone is facing due to privacy violations. For a long time counterfeiting and identity theft have been a problem for many people and without having enough knowledge in technology it makes it harder to avoid this. It's not about being an expert when it comes to these devices but just being able to advance yourself into current events. Now that news and information are not only made for television, we have learned to browse the internet to find the answers ourselves. Everyone has a voice. There's a thin line between having a voice and just saying whatever you want to say. I have said it before, and I will say it again—there's too much of a freedom here. And the lack of discipline drives a community dysfunctional. Without organization and cooperation there is a gap, instantly creating misunderstanding. So many of the social issues that we have today are being brought by our own making. Overtaking the rules won't do any good. They are made for a reason.

The hype has changed over time. A lot of companies are requiring their applicants to complete an online application before passing for an interview. In this age, people are getting more access to information than before. The amount of resources available out there should not be ignored. Research is becoming more and more accessible for those who are conducting theoretical solutions for existing problems. There's no excuse for not paying attention to climate change—not knowing the cause and effect of this global predicament. An issue that should be discussed beyond the classroom. It is not just for the students or environmental groups to debate or march on. This is everyone's problem. We only have one planet and we should do something to preserve it. The use of social media has sparked different organizations in creating awareness campaigns in our society. But more than just creating awareness the use of social media has amplified the connection between people and industry. So many groups are collaborating today in order to maximize their audience. The point of having a channel is to be able to reach out to people and pass on the message that is. These days we have gone from reading magazine and articles online to watching 60 second clip on Facebook about the war in Syria and US election. The events around the world are becoming more impactful to our lives as we see and read about them all the time. Digital media has managed to reach a larger audience when it comes to spreading news, it far surpassed the demand of a local news channel. For the little details like: quick meal preparation, travel, and dating tips. These sorts of questions are searched on Google. Many questions are answered through the search hence news media sites have spread left and right coming from different corners of the world. Credibility of the news is important before buying into their feed. So many of these websites are claiming different angles when it comes to a story. Whether in politics, entertainment or sports there are different sources to get to the latest events. Not to abolish or disregard the print media or postal mail, I actually believe in the advantages and disadvantages of all things. Businesses need more than just one-time exposure for their products. Instead of paying a large sum of money in advertising with less ROI they have learned to partner with other brands for collaboration. In contrary, many of these brick and mortar stores are shutting down. The demand for ecommerce has drastically changed the economy in so many levels. Not only for one industry but with many others. YouTube continues to elaborate its agenda to become a household component by providing the same services like other cable networks but perhaps even better. You might be thinking there is competition but it has always been like that and it can get ugly in the next few years. We can see the cross-culture of brands and products. It is no surprise that social media giants will start releasing their own product line. As a matter of fact, Google is already on its way. With its offering to home technology and voice assistant, we are seeing a promise. But Amazon couldn't sit and watch this happen hence the birth of Alexa. With all of these tools and resources there's no excuse to getting information. But the ability to communicate is going to be in the hands of the people. We write, read, listen, and talk. Being able to start and maintain a conversation is particularly important. In the past, it was customary to give parents a call to check on how they are doing. It doesn't matter if you are in college or living in a different country it would still mean a lot to them to know that somehow you are thinking about them. But as if this is slowly fading away now—which is totally contradicting to the available tools that we have.

When email first came into picture, it led the people from writing traditional letters to typing their keyboards. Although a lot of people still prefer the traditional snail mail, actually they appreciate it more, as what I've heard. I think that's one thing to remember when reaching out to an audience or client. Knowing your demographics can also help you in getting the best results. You see, some CEOs will bother to open their inbox while others don't, and so, if you get a shot you are lucky enough to score a lunch meeting with your potential client. At this time you have to be able to juggle your techniques in terms of business communication. There's formal and informal. Every business is different. Another difference this time is when people don't bother to acknowledge emails. Is this what's happening now? Yes, if you haven't noticed. I guess at first that should mean an implied *Yes* or *No*. But then I thought the opposite. If a person sent an inquiry or maybe a thank you email. It is only polite to at least respond with "*You're Welcome*" then click send. It's not even going to take a minute of your time. That's just me. Now this is where I draw the line because we all get tired of email marketing. At some point that's what we do but the irony of it can sometimes punch us.

It's easy to get caught up with technology these days but that's not all there is. It is only a tool when being used for the benefit of the people. The reason why we have a massive advancement is because of the demand. We wanted a fast and convenient life. We thought of efficiency making things possible through the devices we use, and in some parts is true.

However, it fails to fulfill its promise of communication when the tool itself is misused. Peer to peer interaction brings us closer and with more opportunity to discuss the things that impact us. With many startup companies budding not only in Silicon Valley, leaders are becoming the headliners of their brands. What makes a good leader? It's a question being asked for so many reasons. People are curious how successful leaders have accomplished their goals in life. Same old, same old. They are intrigued about the background story rather than the product. So, when you know it's time to talk about it you should be ready with your own story. Why is it important? There are many answers to that. There are variables to the purpose of a product, but that's the functionality of it. By all means, some of us don't purchase products for utilities but maybe just a guilty pleasure. The consensus of people patronizing brands due to their mission and vision has dramatically changed over the years. On a positive note that means more and more are becoming self-aware of product and demand. It's not a matter of old and new generation. You will see people of all ages in computer and with phones. So that's not part of the equation. It's the messaging. Another irony of the digital age is the measure of reaching people. The substantial truth behind every successful brand is the ability to reach to their audience. Sometimes you don't need a large number of followers or subscribers but giving value to the right audience alone can catapult to a larger scale.

Explore and learn the importance of storytelling. Tell people why your product is important. Give them a chance to get to know your brand on a deeper level. But when you present the purpose, you also accept accountability. There is more than one way of telling why it matters. The ability to create content for a brand is also a big task today. In fact, many of you are monetizing this idea, all you need is an opportunity. The tactics have now changed when call for creative minds started to roll the tide, these influencers have shifted the way promotion and marketing was perceived. Their ability to introduce or compliment a product can be very persuasive to an audience. Sooner or later the demand will only continue to grow and even bigger with an array of platforms to choose from. YouTube has become a very popular destination for reviews, tutorials, and travel escapades brought by the different personalities and curators of style and culture. It is more than just a hobby of getting in front of the camera. But with the realization to become part of a community that cultivates the attention of people to where we are now—the journey begins. Admittedly it is curiosity that points the audience to a channel. Before knowing its content, the audience have already set an expectation to see something different from what they usually watch on television. The creator or vlogger has the overall control of this material.

Whether it's a raw experience or scripted episode—these videos are created with intention and creativity. These types of contents can spark motivation to individuals who are looking for something to inspire them. The world needs more than just ideas but actions from those who want change. Walk the talk. Today content matters. A few news media outlets are able to penetrate the digital market with some contemporary sites to bring a new approach in explanatory journalism. The public pays attention to the things that matter or perhaps that interest them. Some of the nitty-gritty ideas are not only found on big television. Social awareness has also become a key element in branding. Products with purpose. The aim to bring sustainable products to the market is mostly considered by many startups. Allowing them to market their product as environment friendly and energy efficient. Consumers have become wiser when it comes to their household needs.

Although price is another considerable factor, people demand quality while knowing this will cause more. Compatibility and convenience are also very important to customers. Sometimes it's hard to keep up with the changes in our society. But in order to stay in touch with the reality we must do what we can to be informed.

Millennials and entrepreneurs are two of the most commonly used words in the industry today. With most startups being led by those who are in their 20s and 30s there's no surprise that development of their products will most likely to target middle-aged group otherwise the young generation. Although there's no discrimination or any sort into this. It only gives us the projection of where the market is headed. It's better to be prepared. Get your leadership mindset on. Things happened really fast in the market. You have to get in the position already. There's a reason why consumers prefer to shop online—and that's because of time. It's when they can browse through catalogs without the pressure of a salesperson breathing behind their necks. If you are not ready to checkout, you can always go back to it later. Easy and convenient. Amazon has been a game-changer in the ecommerce ecosystem.

The amplification of social media as distribution channels for creators is also another factor. It gathers data for companies to inspect which products are highly popular otherwise bestseller to their customers. Aside of course from looking at the sales, it is important to know what drives the customers to buy that product. It is easier to look at the pattern of where consumerism is headed, because that's where we are going. Those who value the opinion of their customers may be doing it for the right reasons. Feedback is important. It gives the brand its credibility. We heard of there's no such thing as bad publicity. Either way consumers are becoming more vocal to their demands which have helped the decision making of businesses. It may not be able to persuade a certain company to perfect a product or improve customer service, but it's giving other customers the information to help them decide their next purchase. Influence marketing could be just a tool for the people by the people. A good source should command clarity and credibility to its content. Many times scattered information can mislead the audience creating confusion. Utilizing the best tool for communication will allow best results.

In Ancient Egypt, not everyone was mummified. The burial process which made one part of the Egyptian culture rather popular while sensationalized in movies was in fact more of a privilege than tradition. The eviscerated, dried, and bandaged corpse also known as the mummy was an expensive and long process fitted for the wealthy members of the society while others were buried in the depths of desert pits. The distinction of social classes has long existed and even today we battle the idea of equality. Men and women are in tug of war to win the most powerful title. As spectators we feel the urge to support our "person"—a symbolic statue of our group or status. The word status comes present in any situation that calls for classification of a being or an entity.

J.K. Rowling the bestselling author of Harry Potter books has an estimated net worth of $1 billion making her the richest living author in the world today. Although her wealth is a closely guarded secret, she is undeniably one of the most successful and influential authors of this time. Enough to say that she doesn't need reservation to walk into a restaurant.

There's a magnitude of influence a person can have and it's inside in each one of us. Today an individual would say "*I want to make an impact...I want to change the world.*" The stereotypical statement of those who are lost in their own time and space. Those who delve into themselves perhaps looking for their own meaning in life. It is not to discourage them or even yourself, but such lines are becoming trite over time. Make proof. And by that, I don't mean the materialistic side effects of money. Do an action that gives value. Society will judge you but keep going anyway.

Changes in work environment is inevitable as it is part of moving forward. There will always be competition for positions. It is easier to replace a prototype than a product. Even so for a tenure employee—there's no guarantee that such job is kept forever. Learning to adapt to a new environment could be hard or easy. Keeping an open mind is a good way to start.

Every person who wants to be successful in life will have to make sacrifices one way or another. The demands on this path are unpredictable and not simple. It is the total opposite of what other people think of building businesses these days. Without thinking deeply or knowing the consequences that will soon arise when managing your own brand. But short-term goals do sound fun, exciting, and reckless at times.

Some ten or fifteen years ago email was an exciting remedy to what was a developing mind in the age of computer communication. With a simple click and little bit of typing you can be in touched with anyone in the world, although it was originally embraced for personal use—checking an inbox would mean anticipation for an answer, an acknowledgement to an inquiry and sometimes a simple *Hello*. And for a moment it was a cautious sign that letters and birthday cards might soon vanished in the hype of electronic greetings and postcards. It was also a polite gesture to send a reply message after reading the email to which today has extended to five days later and for some never mind. It has become a prerogative to reply to an email.

When business email came into picture people somewhat obligated themselves to bring their jobs anywhere they go. It was a blessing and curse at the same time. Teddy who was in Hawaii for a vacation that he didn't have in almost five years was in a conference meeting. He ended up booking the next flight to go back to New York. As crazy as it is the world is changing fast and it's up to you if you want to get on the ride or be left out.

It may seem like a force that is pulling us towards a new dimension. This is where all people communicate with their phones, tablets, and bluetooth devices. Maybe we can all relate when that day comes. But I wouldn't wish that to happen. I actually like the classic version of let's-have-coffee-sometime. The sit down conversation between two or more people sharing ideas while enjoying food and drinks in a not so expensive restaurant. I'd like to think of the regular days when we don't have to check our phones and emails every minute and be able to have peace of mind from everything. But that's almost difficult these days unless you are seventy-five-years-old in a retirement home. Every person who has a phone is able to connect to the internet. So as not necessarily having someone to talk to but sometimes a self-indulgence or some sort. Having a phone or computer gives you an access to the world.

Information is a distraction. A disguised truth that leads from one end to another. Our brain exerts chemical components as it functions, while brain activity dictates our actions it can easily get destructed. As this happens we lose our focus. We are all probably guilty with this. One time you could be reading an article, searching Google, watching YouTube, is that a 50% off deal, click on that too and browse on Amazon. This could take a while and I can go on and on. The next thing you know you've spent about forty-five minutes to an hour fooling around the web while you have work to do. I don't know if you've noticed this but somehow the brain has ways of telling us if it needs a break or something. Taking short breaks allows it to relax and regain its focus that affects our productivity. According to Centers for Disease Control and Prevention, there are 4.4 million youth ages 4-17 in the United States that have been diagnosed with ADHD. As researchers from MIT continue to find ways to understand this type of disorder and ways to approach it—they have found out that brain processes information in different ways. And anything that stands out or different from the rest is likely to grab our attention. So, if you see yourself clicking from one website to another—that's all part of the process. For now, people find the satisfaction from shopping online where they can choose and purchase a product anywhere in the world and even the smallest things that can be found in the store probably two blocks away. Those companies make a good fortune of money for all the products and services they provide us. A whole new wave of demands are created. So you'll be the judge to what value they bring especially when you're subscribed to a Premium Plan. They say in life you get what you pay for—and true to almost everything. The idea we have when it comes to technology is all about access and innovation.

With the industry giants such as Amazon, Walmart, and Google, the possibilities are beyond reach. Online shopping has become more than just a past time for some people but a habit or go to resource for those who refuse to mingle in the busy section of the department store. But as customer service is gradually deflating most consumers are becoming more aware and cautious of what they buy online. Knowing that it could take more than just seven business days to hear from a representative. Returns and exchange can be of a hassle and quite frankly nobody wants to do it. So, here we are with the new solution through virtual reality. No, we are not talking about the virtual reality product from Samsung or Google, but V-Commerce. Imagine yourself walking inside Walgreens or Target. Wherein you can seemingly touch and scan your grocery just as like you are physically present in the store. If the VR technology can take us to the hype of a roller coaster ride, stargazing and safari then perhaps it also needs to expand its compartment for the avid shoppers out there. So many discussions and it raises so many questions about how our brain controls our attention and focus. But think of this, if you based your focus into Science, you're going to put yourself into a loop. Your hustle is not going to be mandated based on how your brain works. See it as a subjective intuition that pushes yourself towards performance and hard work. If you want something in life that bad, you'll do all good things possible to get there. It's not simple, it's not easy—but it's not impossible. We've seen it everyday, people who've accomplished their goals, reached their destinations and still going. Don't go at ease, that's going to be your enemy. When you start to feel comfortable you'll slow down. In your mind you're close to achieving it, and it's okay to take a break. Yes, it is not a race— but unless you've already won, I say keep moving.

Our mere purpose of living is to find its meaning. And for some of you who don't read between the lines the harder it is. We find short-term happiness in different forms. Those that are transitory. In some parts we are aware of it but we'd like to escape reality therefore we tolerate such things.

By now we should be able to distinguish the tangibles versus intangibles in our lives. We may not have experienced it all but even fiction is telling us there will always be consequences to whatever we do and no matter what. So, what do we do? We either make good or bad choices—it's up to us. Our actions are only limited when we stop. Although the question lies on its purpose. So the way we see ourselves now in the midst of technology is a projection of consciousness. We certainly enjoy the accessible transportation—thanks to Uber. While all these things are fighting for our attention. We have to evaluate ourselves on what matters. What do we need at this point? What is needed? What is necessary? As we continue to find the true meaning of existence we battle ourselves against the elements of the earth. For what we hold today are the fragments of tomorrow. We slowly realize the most important things in life. And there we hope to find happiness.

It is a rewarding feeling especially to share it with the ones you love. We seek for answers and guidance. That a piece of what we do maybe relevant to the next generation. An aim to put a dent in the universe. It is a challenge but not impossible. There will always be a competition in everything that you do. If you are not competing with anyone at least with yourself. Think of it as a driving force that pushes you to the limit. All the different ideas you have in mind are waiting to explode. They come alive as you stood up in the pedestal. The question: How bad do you want it? Always on top of the class. As a professional you seek the recognition. The approval. Yes, it is a mitigated truth. But every individual, at some point, wants that acknowledgment which is a rewarding feeling. There is curiosity and thirst for change. For what we value we preserve. We strive to maintain if not develop it. For technology in itself is evolving. Nothing is permanent.

I remember the time I switched from YahooMail to Gmail some years ago. I really didn't have any specific reason except that I wanted to create a Google account for the heck of it since that was the new thing. Like it won the popularity contest. But I guess people saw it coming then, the premonition became a reality. Google took its spot being the internet giant. It wasn't that Yahoo completely sucked at its game, in fact it worked so hard to deliver as many information as it could—a summary that is found on their homepage. While Google kept it plain and simple. So I thought about it, the difference between the two wasn't just about the amount of information as well as the capacity in organization. Yahoo back then was more like the Yellow Pages. It was the catalog of many things from entertainment, sports, news and so on. Today it's more like a digital magazine of highlighted stories. On the other hand, Google has projected itself to be the library of information—its version of encyclopedia. It aims to analyze and categorize everything according to its content. But what got the most of us was its ranking system. Now every business or personal profile prides itself when it shows up on top of the search results. It has become the target for marketing—to be on top of Google search.

One of the myths in SEO is that of blog content—that it will give you traffic and gain audiences. But it's not that simple, especially if you don't have the site credibility. Reading is a challenging battle for everyone. It's not about the short attention span but a key factor that is interest. For a person who has no interest in a certain topic won't waste time reading the material. But the exemption comes in visualization. People who watch videos, talks and demonstration tend to pay more attention to the matter. We get excited about social experiments, parody and spoofs. It's showing a different take to dealing with reality or simply making fun of the situation. Since insult became an amusement for those who are looking for a good laugh—it's a backward step to social behavior and to what defines "fun." To have an option allows us to choose on what we think is for the best of our interests. But again, information is a destruction, so we go back to getting attention and how to focus on things that are more important to us.

I believe that we can program our minds and condition it the way we want it to. For example, if I wanted to write an article, I will have to do things that are only related to what I am doing, all the rest must be disregarded. In an article by Dr. Julie Schwartzbard on a website called BetterMind, there are three different types of attention that are producing the ability to focus and concentrate. The following are:

(1)   *Selective attention.* To focus on one thing while shutting down the other areas.

(2)   *Divided attention.* It is like multi-tasking, when you are able to do two or more things at the same time.

(3)   *Sustained attention.* Being able to stay focus on a single thing or subject for a long time. You don't get easily destructed with things around you.

When you believe in yourself that you can do it—you will. Someone once said that suffering could bring forth potential. Pain can sometimes serve as motivation. It all depends on how a person takes the loss. Learn not to complain in life. You must understand sadness for you to appreciate happiness.

The pressure that social media brings into our lives is sometimes irrelevant. When everything seems to be publicized, it's hard to find authenticity in every person. An exemption for the brands as it is part of what they do. Although brands are psychoanalyzing the consumers using algorithms that would somehow provide them data to capture, predict, and suggest next purchase. The result depends on consumer behavior.

Permission and Privacy

People will talk about you one way or the other. They don't need your permission. The obstructive truth is biased. At some point they only want you to see what you want to see, or what they want you to see. Some social media sites or apps will give you an option to put your account in public or private. Although changing it to private forfeits the purpose of social media itself.

There's conflict on projection. Of what is being made to believe. Seeing social media as universal platform for everyone. A step to breaking barriers to a place where free-thinkers and thought leaders are observed. The notion to connect people and culture. Yes, there is that. Those who celebrate the idea of one world as well as curious to one's culture and the others. How interesting to be able to talk to different people from different parts of the world? To family and friends. That communication is already an accessible unit to mankind. The same reason, however, it is a challenge to refine the contents of these channels. But regardless, people who are in search for sense of belonging choose to join the group.

To Become an Influence

A relatively simple word with an illustrated meaning of what is suggested. A lot of these startups today are somewhat delivering a statement that for whatever reason they do what they do to put a dent in the universe, if not change the world. Of course, that's a long way to go. For those who dare to fill the shoes in the likes of Steve Jobs and Mark Zuckerberg.

The incurable aspirations of the young generation to follow the footsteps of the great leaders in the history. And not only to speak about technology but to any field that is. A motivation that has shifted in ways that would continue to challenge the idea of learning outside the four walls in campus. Dropping out of college is an alternate route or risk to take in order to pursue one's dream. Perhaps an inadvertent cliché', but I'd say this again—education is eternal.

The rules of advertising and marketing might have changed since the birth of social media. At least society is not oblivious to that. Meanwhile, tv commercials seem to lean toward melodramatic, confusing, and oddly messaging. In an attempt to fight for attention with ways that could tickle one's interest. Advertising industry spends billions of dollars. Surely, a more convenient reason for big companies to pay a huge sum during the Superbowl. One of those big events where people actually watch television. In less than ordinary days most of us are tuned in to our phones. But those who understood change are willing to adapt in a growing culture.

Supposedly prime etiquette and courtesy are still being practiced by some people or in that case the management itself. If you're going out of town you would want to stay in some place where accommodation is not overrated. At the end of the day, we expect a great customer service. A way of an indirect commercial but showcasing what they can offer coming from a different perspective. An article from Business Insider talks about how Airbnb could slow down the growth of hotel revenues by 80%. This time hotels should be more open to possibilities that entertainment is not the only way to get their customers rather than focusing on a single market, they should allow other potential partners in transcending the message. Be competitive and friendly at the same time.

What is the Food Concept?

A good recipe is needed for a successful campaign. Ingredients are the components. How is it beneficial to the people? If you have a platform that serves an intended purpose, you must also learn to evaluate its value.

The Trojan War was one of the most significant events in Greek history—it showed the art of winning a battle. And by the use of that symbolic horse that brought waged to the city of Troy a methodical attack took place. The same can be said prior to launching a product. One should be able to gather audience months before to spark the anticipation.

Where everyone is—you're there. So they say never underestimate the power of bad publicity. And that there's no such thing. The commercial industry highlights the consumption of people. What is a commodity? Some of these things probably don't even apply to our everyday lives. Social issues are eventful.

Traditional news carry on the core values of mass media. Where content serves information and knowledge to the public.

Social media has played roles in different aspects of this time. The components are their own tools, of which became the bridge to communication. Such a torn for a channel between documenting and creating. Also, one thing to remember is that an audience is not only an audience. They are also learners. There is an underlying truth of motivation. People watch travel videos because they are naturally beautiful. It catches the interest of the mind. Plus, it takes them to a place they haven't been before. It gives them an idea of environment and people. Perhaps where hospitality is not an overrated idea.

In the last two decades innovation has practically changed the way we make use of technology and looking forward to the future. More than the expansion of tech giants, the reception of the public has changed toward the capabilities and influence of the worldwide web. Business owners are becoming more knowledgeable when it comes to the placement and distribution of their products. In reality, one can simply sign up and create a seller account on Amazon to start selling. And this has virtually changed the landscape of entrepreneurship. Somehow it managed to eliminate the gatekeepers of this industry. The internet has basically given the people the opportunity to create, earn, and build. So many of these things around us today didn't make sense twenty years ago. No one would have paid attention to it. However, the rising demand of information and communication tools has become the invoice of these platforms. User-generated contents are great source of monetizing a channel. This is not limited to a single entity which means everyone can hustle their way in creating a brand.

Good Stewardship

Getting as many work experiences as early as possible will harness your skills. Back then I took two internships in media at the same time. I knew I was not going to get paid but I showed up to work on the weekends as I was scheduled. Sacrifice is an important quality in order for us to take the steps in accomplishing our goals. Expect the roads to be bumpy. You won't get to rub elbows with the big bosses right on the first time. You will work an entry level job to see and understand the structure of labor and not just the company itself. A tendency of forgetting about the frontliners can sabotage one's leadership skills. Regardless of the industry you are working in, there is a need for good leaders. Not only the Presidents and CEOs but as well as the supervisors and team leaders. Every staff is a leader. A title only lives up to itself when the function is done. The idea of everyone working together is positive. It welcomes all types of work that will help an organization thrive. A good leader will take time to introduce himself and speak to his people. Even though he didn't have it on schedule. At the end of the day we all need a pat on the back. Being able to decide not only for yourself but for other people who are depending on you is yet more than just a task. It's a responsibility. Leaders who are privileged enough to make decisions would implement measures necessary for the company. The market does not forgive. One mistake can affect a lot of people.

It's easy to say "*that's not my job because I am the boss*" but that's basically the point. With your position you have the authority to make things happen and make things right. I have watched a couple of people who were incapable of this situation. I thought to myself it deprives those who are willing and more qualified to represent. There are different types of leaders but those who see themselves as one of the people may not have the right courage to take on the job. It is a valuable nature to be able to associate yourself with other co-workers but at one point they need a person to take action for them, and that person is you. You can talk to them and shake their hands but remember your title. A good leader inspires the people to be the best version of themselves. He does not discount accountability and responsibility. Instead he or she encourages. Aside from helping you fulfill your duties, he or she trains you to be able to share the same knowledge to your other co-workers. The ability to look after the herd and not one sheep. It allows to have a sense of conduct and communication spread through work environment as it is needed. Staff will learn the technical skills of work that they need by training, however the concept of co-working with others is another task for them. Today employees will not work for the same job for years unlike in the past. It's not the entitlement but more of an option to where they would like to go. The young generation are risk takers. They are always looking for adventure. They are passionate about making changes or improvement to their own environment. They crave for creativity and hustle. Some things that perhaps they don't probably feel or experience in another traditional work setting. These are the type of people who don't just settle for the check.

Self-awareness will lead you to obstacles and happiness. While both worlds collide differently it reveals the truth behind your work and purpose. There's no greater joy to being able to work on something that you love to do. In the meantime, we do what we have to do. There is no disregard to your work. Some say they choose to stay with their job because it pays the bills. Ambition is going to drive you even farther. While your potential is your motivation. People see the best of themselves when they accomplish one thing and another. Somehow it gives them hope and vision of possibilities. That's why it's important to know what you really want to do. If what you are doing makes you happy. Are you looking at the long-term venture or temporary excursion? Exploring these ideas and options will eventually guide you to a new path. You may also have to evaluate the things around you. What are you good at? A person is likely to succeed by taking action and not only by ideas. Taking a leap in your life is yet another chance you would want to take. With the advancement in our world, anyone should take that first step to moving forward. There's an opportunity that's waiting ahead of you, but only by chance that you will discover the possibility.

Reaction to Society

Post a question in one of those forum sites to see what type of answers you'll get. It's another form of discourse. Whether the saying was true or not—it started a conversation. The only demand there is time. There's no guarantee that you'll get the response right away or just before you needed it. There's a catch to all these things. But what makes social media work is the ability to distribute lines of information and statements that can be of anybody's interest. Forget the analytics for the meantime. If this was not all about marketing the idea would totally lie on communication. If there's more to that, maybe we're missing on something. In 2001, Wikipedia sought the demand for encyclopedic information that would allow people to find centralized information based on the current events. But while it can reconstruct ideas, history, and other puzzle pieces—there was a question of integrity and credibility amongst sources. Gaining so much attention from its platform as well as competition was undeniable proving it was more than a fad for others—it became a tool at some point and even today people still use it. Getting social seems like another approach to being relevant to people with the use of these tools. Whatever and whoever is note-worthy gets the spotlight. The use of social media from political groups have also been criticized using the platform for propaganda and nothing less. Although other organizations have swiftly cultivated certain movements gathering support from the public through the magnitude of social networking. These types of responses urged a sentiment for change and equality. A cry for reason and purpose of what they believe is right. It was not as active as it was twenty years ago. People simply would want to befriend you on social media in the hope of finding another lost soul and perhaps more than that. There is a connection of collected experiences within these groups and for their voices to be heard is something the world has never seen before. Without any approval from the media or other authoritative organizations social groups are not afraid of marching their way down the streets, crossing arms and waving signs. They remain synchronized as far as the topic, plea or even the symbolic colors of the movement. When you go on Instagram or Twitter you will easily find these groups through their hashtags—with that you can contemplate on whether you want to be a part of it too. So many of these movements are calling for attention and awareness. The ALS Association reportedly made up to $115 million after the challenge has gone viral on the internet. It also garnered a lot of support from celebrities who participated and took the challenge. All of this was again spread out through social media. These challenges are another way of reaching out to the community by asking them into participating. So that's the upside of it.

Utilizing resources not only for your own benefit will eventually give you a good harvest. What do I mean by that? It simply means good karma. Doing it for the right reason will set you and your business apart. The importance of giving value is a tremendous part to your success. Realizing there is more to just selling products or the brand as a whole. So much are only substantial to what could be a real mission inside. There's a need for us to be awaken when we are doing things. We don't do them for the sake of doing them. That's an obligation. But to do an act with purpose. That's different. You can call it passion. You can call it service. But whether or not we take action, the world will continue to move forward. Changes are within the environment. And when you are part of that environment you have an opportunity to be a part of that change.

When you open up your mind to the greater calling, there's a certain force that pulls you toward it. We all have heard of the Law of Attraction. Now I'm not an expert when it comes to meditation or any metaphysical attributes that allow positive energy to come into an individual. But what I know is this— you can make things happen. Taking an action is a powerful remark to fulfilling your destiny. Think deeper and see for what truly is your passion.

As a former correspondent I like the cheap thrills of seeing my name the next morning on printed newspaper. At the end, I didn't see it as a waste of time because I knew I was going to get something. It was all the experience. It was knowing a little bit about the industry. That many people still yearn for that piece of information to be given to them. To know that you are doing something different, something you like. And in the process, I thought to myself if I enjoy what I do. Making a decision that can possibly change your life forever is intimidating.

Often times we do things that are easy for us. It's like an escape. But only that we are forced to do so. In contrary that is not the case for all. Where there is vision, there is hope. It is possible to pursue your dreams. It is possible to make something for yourself. There's nothing wrong with that. You dream and live on. But don't just live by, there's a difference. Shakespeare said "*nothing is good or bad but thinking makes it so.*" Without action your ideas will remain in place. Do something. There is going to be a lot of criticism when you first take the step. They're not going to like it. You don't expect them to be your supporters right away. But it's not about them. It's about what you do. There is a vision in every one of us. Believe that you have one too.

Social platforms exist due to the demand of the society. The transitional effect appears to have influenced the psychological function for all of us—those who are using and capitalizing on social media. Yes, there is an explanation behind every click and like. Psychologists are also looking into the side effects of too much engagement on the internet. Of course, the studies have been around for years now since they start to notice the hook. For the most part the idea of internet is connectivity. You get connected whenever you go online and search for information. You get connected when you comment on a post. It is somehow urging for participation. It commands action. And words will become content. The explanation of cause and effect. Why do people do what they do? What is the purpose of it? Anomaly. That certain point is given to you to expand horizons. Truth of the matter is everyone needs an opportunity. You have to start somewhere. Don't expect investors coming to you when you're building your startup. There's too much pressure on creating a project that is built for others. Focus on its value. What value can you give to the audience and your future clients?

Identifying the purpose of the project is inevitable. The creation is not only for fun. There must be an underlying emphasis to what it stands for and the story behind it. The call to action is going to be the game changer. Startups are moving too fast these days jumping into conclusion. There's a difficult choice for those who may have less experience. Good intentions my friend. You will be rewarded for the good things that you have done. Learn to adapt to your environment. Trust me you will need it later on and in so many ways. Business etiquette is important. Communication is a two-way street.

"The entitled generation," a rueful Ernest Hemingway might have written today, as subtitle to an elaborate ode of despondency. Whereas, a new cohort of ambivalent minds are lurking in spread at the corporate spaces to advance their demands without prior engagements. In some ways they were led to believe that "everything must be handed to them" or perhaps that hardwork is an overrated standard for prosperity. There is no sentiment for a position that was already called for even before they set foot into something. As middle-class Americans won't expect much from a politician born with a silver spoon. Although, one shoe doesn't fit all. A suggestion that certain practices are used to establish connections in much appreciated ways. A study about millennials pointed that they do well by doing good. Whether the being was to uplift the common norm of young leaders, there may be some truth to this. It's called the social mindset, whereas, millennials are known to be masters of digital communication. And for whatever reason they get the work done when praised. As it is with other groups.

There was a time when college students would fight for an internship at Goldman Sachs or Ernst and Young. And that environmental field trip showing they volunteered to put as social activity. All this is part of building a solid resume so when the time comes, they can present themselves as rightful candidate.

But recent study shows this is no longer true as far as the millennials are concerned. Aside from choosing the kind of job they want, other opportunities including company benefits are being considered during the job hunt. They don't flatter themselves when they are commended for an academic achievement, however, believing that they deserved it so. The challenge for the most part is adjustment.

Being able to work for a company of your dreams is supposedly a fulfillment that drives an individual to want more and achieve goals for the future. And to what extent that some of these millennials would go for a high position without realizing the prior qualifications. Not because one can simply Google and download data from the internet to make him appear like a better employee compared to someone who has worked for more than ten years in the field. There may be a debate between the skill gap and qualifications for these individuals, but one couldn't care less of what was being commanded in a job.

Somehow it tells them that other jobs can be found anywhere, and so, there's no rush and need to be stuck in the same cubicle when they can run for a walk-in interview the next day. They say that being a leader has nothing to do with your rank. It can happen to certain people who hold the true value of leadership and it is more than just an authority. Although being the President or CEO of your company feels the need of leading the flock. But what it means to be a leader remains to be a question.

Like any business there are financial challenges that can determine its direction. Whether you let the entire boat sink or throw some people in the water. But it's easier to look at the other way and stand up for the best interest of the many. Everyone has a choice. When you do be sure to make the right one.

Travel while you can, if you can. There's more to what you see beyond naked eyes. There's more to the world. To be discovered. If you have the chance to see the other side of it, you'll find out that life is beautiful and meaningful.

Being productive and creative can be a tall order whether you have a regular job or running a business. Time and quality are needed for best results. But with the fast pace equation of the everyday demands, how are you able to keep up.

The demanding job could be the main source of the problem. Some studies showed that 74% of private company staff are not happy or dissatisfied with their jobs. When being asked of why they choose to stay—there was a common answer, and that is difficulty in finding another job. Or otherwise the threat of unemployment. They would rather stay at the same workplace and deal with their everyday challenge than finding a new start with no certainty. According to sources, when people are stressed out, they are unable to perform well not only at work but life in general.

What's more important? In work-life balance schedule. We've heard so many stories on how work can be overwhelming it's completely taking over your life. Well here's the problem—you are not taking action. If you are no longer happy with your career then perhaps it's time to consider another path. Millennials these days are easily burnt out with the challenges of corporate lifestyle—it's just given. But in fact, this is also true amongst other individuals regardless of their schedule. Productivity at work can be stressful especially when you're trying to beat the deadline, a part of the company culture. But some of these organizations today are also trying to cope when it comes to accommodating the needs of their employees—being able to give them a more rewarding experience at work.

Elevate yourself. Not only with the things that you are good at. But continue to be challenged to pursue your great potential. Practice makes it perfect. Perfecting the ideal. The complexity of being able to balance your time within the family and work can be overwhelming. For some startups being in a limited space depending on their product category will play an advantage of utilizing resources and handling co-workers. But it doesn't discount responsibility of overseeing the people that are part of the model. What does it take to create a fun-loving environment for your employees? Whether you are managing a small business or not, there is a responsibility to fill being a leader. A concept of providing the people both their needs and wants is not such a bad idea. Setting good example of fulfillment and vision is an effective way to promote fun and productive work environment.

When I started as a local reporter for a daily newspaper, I had my share of facing deadlines. Often and not, there were stories that cannot be put off for another day which means for a breaking news it needs to be current, as it should be. Having been to attend press conferences and launching I have always felt the inviting atmosphere of society willingly open to be explored and cultivated. I was amazed by the fast-changing revolution of technology, design, communication, and social media. Needless to say we have all the resources that we need in order for us to pursue and utilize our skills. There's no excuse only execution. I believe that if you're good enough in what you do, you will be rewarded. Do it for the right reason. Whatever you are passionate about. Do it because it makes you happy. It makes you excited to start your day.

SELECTED FORMS

Almost 500 km away from the seaside, you can hear every rush on the shore. Chills in the morning greet you with wonder as the sunlight hits the bream this one is for everyone to see. A small town in Aberdeen, shows this little traditional place you could stay just to have a breath of fresh air and far from the rumbling chaos in the city. Set on top of the hill where it has been for a long time and waiting for a visit of those who may be lost or looking for peace and just to watch the scenery. Where you could lay in the sand and stare through the sky. A monotonous being probably won't complain as this would be an imagination for a while.

(i) It's time for change up in the workplace. One thing I realized is that in order for a person to be excited with just about anything and everything that he does, an anticipation sort of an imagination must be present—if not created to raise the levels of intuition and participation in our body. Otherwise there's no thrill. This is somewhat important to work environment. Millennials these days are big on exploration and adventure. They cannot be tied up around their desks. They dread the 8-to-5 routine and perhaps a lot of people do. It's a given fact that needs no further detailing. But the excitement actually allows no opportunities for creativity and productivity and this happens when your workplace is built with character and functionality. Aside from modern offices, industrial and urban feel type of designs are definitely inviting to staff and even visitors. Not only it gives an appeal to a company, it also helps the employees to perform well with their tasks given the free-flowing working space.

(ii) An ode to yourself. There are many reasons why one should be excited to get up in the morning and go to work. First, you love your job—and that's basically it. When you're contented enough and happy with what you do everything else follows. No, it's not the food chain but evidently a reaction to environment. As an employee you can only strive for greatness in a career choice or so-called profession that you choose. It pays the bills. In reality every individual seeks an opportunity to better himself. But when there's fear, it overshadows the possibilities that there might be something bigger out there.

It's taking a leap. Although not too many people are in favor of taking risks not especially when it comes to their jobs, there must be a better way of finding your niche and to discover what is it that you like to do. Sometimes you have to constantly ask these questions in order for you to justify the situation. It works for the most part. Even if there's uncertainty when your mind is wired on perseverance and chances, you'll find yourself ready to jump. It's not going to be easy at first but that's just part of the bargain. You are responsible for your future. And so, with all the decision-making that you do, you must be willing to accept both failure and success. The road maybe a little narrow at first and that's okay when you're sharpening your skills you need to be wiser than before. Believe that you can and you will. There's a strong friction that accompanies every action. Soon enough when you look back, it's all worth it.

Allow yourself to find distance whether in place or not you have to breathe for a minute. Let there be a reflection of your thoughts and hopes whichever they may be, there's that one goal you would want to do and before it's too late you have to embark on a journey that might just set you free. Living things behind is the first step to moving forward. Look for the things that satisfy your soul and uplifts your spirit. Many of us don't find the time to explore but for those who are doing it, go on and continue. With the hopes of finding reality and truth. A surprising event perhaps that awaits each and everyone of us. Being relentless in many ways can only make you stronger like waves crushing through the shore.

From coast to coast we travel to collect data and capture different pictures that tell story behind the lenses. One thing that gets me excited in every click of the camera is being able to preserve that particular motion and time of which cannot be repeated. A very special feeling when you have that authority to command a certain image that will live to illustrate such beauty and scenery. In most cases you would want to document your travels as you scour through the cities and downtown strip with locales and delicacies that are somehow unfamiliar. Perhaps a dance to the tune of their culture that's different from what you're used to. But isn't that the purpose? Carry your camera at all times for you don't know what you can capture. The most fun memories and instant moments that can only be relived through the lenses—and behind is the story.

(iii) Interestingly our culture has somewhat embraced the social phenomenon brought to us by the independent film makers, travelers, vloggers who are eager and determine to create their own adventure—it's hard not to appreciate. Not only celebrated by pop culture or the millennials, some of the most inspiring stories are found in the most uneasy and unexpected places. These are the encounters that made the background of every shot, for every captured moment is another story to tell. Getting that inspiration is but one click away. The spirits of these individuals are so inviting the photographs are speaking by themselves.

(iv) Leave your mark and share your passion. The art is calling and it takes more than a creative soul to express the beauty that lies within. For every stroke could be an anecdote to a story. It paints both joy and sorrow that no one else could see. The special bond between you and the canvass is taken into account. There goes a time that an individual will have to expand his horizon and spread wings for the future. Art is for us. An interpreted meaning that is beyond the lines and hues to fuel the mind.

(v) It is undeniable that technology has ruled people's time for nature and other recreational activities, not unless of course if you don't enjoy a day of pressing keys or taking selfies. There's nothing to be mad about technology because one way or another it has helped us. The advancement is only an idea, but execution is dependable to its user. So, while cyber bullying is continuously affecting society, not to mention school environment. If we only take responsibility with every action using the tools we have, not allowing disrespect or contempt, to dismiss any abusive behavior, we can somehow coexist. People carry their phones everyday. As if waiting for that single moment to capture an event no matter good or bad, somehow urging them the need to document the action. Anything could happen on a given day and when you get to see something extraordinary you wouldn't pass on that chance.

The Age of Communication

The shape of social communication is continuously changing that we have to learn our ways through it. As humans we learn to adapt to our own environment and whether we like it or not we live in a digital age. As the rules of advertising and marketing have long changed since the birth of social media, it is necessary to be able to adapt on what drives an audience to a certain product. Where do we go from here? If you are familiar with the food concept then you might as well treat your social media accounts as such. Find the right ingredients first, cook them well, and serve.

On the other side startups are only utilizing what they have as far as resources. You do what is necessary and essential to your business. If you have to play the game then probably you should of course with rules intended. Knowing your target audience is a must. It helps when engaging to what they find interesting. Content matters. In so many ways you can put it but that should be relevant on establishing a brand.

Taking action is literally—taking action. A lot of times the problem is not being able to do, but not doing it at all. There's a difference. Try to make sense of it. Reflect on yourself with whatever you are doing. If your career is important to you— ask yourself *why*. With this, another question comes next and before you know it the answer is right in front of you. Don't waste your time and do more of the things that really matter. Take action.

The first step to become successful is execution. Sometimes we need a little pat on the back—a sign that we are somehow appreciated. There are certain things in life that just come and go. But when you've worked hard for something you feel the need to be recognized. Even the little side-notes from your supervisor saying that you did a great job can be an uplifting feeling.

In 2016, there were rumors about an acquisition of Twitter Inc. Of course, the stock market went up and down crazy and now leaping to 2018, the social media platform that is mostly popularized by one political figure no less than the President of the United States is being scrutinized again. This time based on The Harris Poll survey, in which they examined some of the most on-demand social media platforms and how do Americans really feel about them. Twitter is leading the pack with 46% votes saying "Kill it and hope it dies" while 43% believes that it should stay and the remaining 11% are not familiar.

Whether or not you've used Twitter before or any social media platform on that note, there is a sense of influence and community that is being formed within this space. The idea of social media is not just to promote oneself, if you're a celebrity or business, but to share ideas and topics that concern the society. As intriguing as it has become throughout these years the age of social media has become a vital component in releasing news and information to the public. Where people are not only relying to watching television broadcast or radio—they scroll on their phones or listen to podcasts while riding the subway or during break time (if there's any). That's just the reality of it.

Although millions of Americans use social media every day at some point they wish they didn't have to deal with it. However, a 40-year-old teller wouldn't want to be left behind on what is happening in culture and entertainment. The fastest way to find out is through online. Another reason also why our phone is by far the most important handheld device. It is difficult to keep up with technology at times but the challenge comes to its user and application.

The digital age is slowly taking over. Apart from the increasing usage of artificial intelligence (AI) when it comes to technology devices and machinery—there is no surprise that video gaming is now considered as mental health condition. Word Health Organization (WHO) has called the condition as "gaming disorder"—where there is impairment in personal, family and social functioning and lack of communication and behavioral patterns that are significantly disabling the individual. Video gaming can take a toll on a person's daily life jeopardizing other priorities and learning skills. The World Health Assembly has also listed the disorder on its forthcoming 11th International Classification of Diseases. According to Nielsen, the average U.S. gamer age 13 or older spent 6.3 hours a week in 2013. But it's not only the time that is being counted—other concerns raised amongst parents with their children being constantly online, is the violence of the game they play. Although different non-profit organizations have released campaigns to promote safety internet environment there is no assurance to this. It was tackled before that young teenagers even adults are being addicted to playing video games which resulted to unhealthy lifestyle and unlikely character of being isolated inside his or her own reality another threat has showed up according to reports. (*This article also appeared on ChicagoTribune.com*)

If things are not falling into place and we just want to hit the brick wall it could be a sign of stress. But think again, researchers have found another way to embrace this unnerving feeling that constantly shakes the person inside of us whether it's work-related or personal. Not knowing how to handle stress is a problem because it gets a person out-of-focus and simply uninspired.

Challenges and meaningful encounters in our lives are brought by stress, or in some part. You may not know this but being stressed can only make you stronger, smarter and more confident to take on the lead. Think of it as your breaking free moment from the comfort zone—where your relentlessness and intuition can be tested.

Kelly McGonigal a lecturer from Stanford and program developer for Stanford Center for Compassion and Altruism Research and Education once said that stress is not always harmful. Sometimes a person needs to embrace both the good and bad in life experiences. There's no way of telling you'd like to keep the same job for the next 10 years or pursue another career choice—and by that perhaps to follow your true calling. These days millennials are judged by their lack of discipline, entitlement and poor choices that could only be some of the pinpointing list of how they carry themselves in our ever changing and disaffected society.

Instead of seeing stress as an enemy treat it as a training ground to better yourself, to outdo what needs to be done. Yes, stress could be another version of yourself that's only pushing you to the limit. But mind you that's only to your own prerogative. It's just how you see things from inside and out— and when you make the most out of it you'll soon find the true key in succeeding the battles set forth. You are challenged.

Habits are more like daily routines. What we are used to doing everyday. It allows ourselves to repeat or maintain an action that needs to be done. There are good habits and bad habits. Although they don't necessarily define your objectives in life, they can affect the progress and it matters. Most people probably don't pay attention to their habits. For that reason it is important that we evaluate our actions. And not only that we also need to examine our thoughts and words for they are all connected.

In Time and With Water

This story previously appeared on Chicago Tribune.

THEN FOUR WEEKS LATER he found himself looking for a pair of scissors to carve a hole on his belt giving it a notch tighter. He now had lost forty pounds. While getting ready for work in the morning he would wear his favorite button-down long sleeve. A fitted large size that used to trace his proportions of muscles became a mere oversized shirt hanging an extra space. Seven years ago, this feeling would have given him a sense of satisfaction but not anymore. At 38 he is only starting his life. A husband and father to a beautiful little girl.

He didn't have this kind of fear before. He fears for his life now. "*I don't want to die.*"

In a revelation to his family. He started purging food in the extreme means to lose and control weight. For over twenty years he has continued the bad habit that could cause his life. He didn't have a full grasp of the consequences until the night he spat blood while he stroked his index and middle fingers down his throat. At this point he flushed the toilet but vomit stains remained including the half-digested food he just consumed two hours ago.

He looked at himself in the mirror. The reflection showed a 310-pound stout build man. A face he had been staring for years and since he started to hide himself in the bathroom to get rid of the nutriment. Nobody really knew. From the outside no one would think that he has bulimia nervosa. At five feet ten inches tall he currently weighs 140 pounds, which is less than half of his size seven years ago. He seems to be in a good shape.

Andre, has stalwart rationality when it comes to his eating disorder, a security analyst who looks like an ordinary guy from a distance. Andre drives a 2015 Chevrolet Colorado and listens to hip hop while he enjoys jazz occasionally. He used to go out fishing at the lake on the weekends. He said he was good at it. By the suggestion of his psychologist to give him something to do. It was an activity that would help ease his mind, and not to wallow in self-pity. He particularly didn't like him but he took his advice anyway. It worked for a couple of months then he stopped.

He never really liked going to the doctor. Although Dr. Avinash was different. He thought he was that kind of a doctor who really paid attention to a patient, like himself, but he didn't feel a connection with him being his counselor. "I don't see the point of telling some stranger about how I throw up to keep my weight and not be fat," Andre said. An imagination that his confession is going to be ridiculed and probably worth sharing to amuse a small group in therapy or intervention, surrounded by those who are suffering the same illness.

"No, I don't want that," Andre shook his head.

Another thing is that of him being a male. Andre out of curiosity did his own research and found the neglect of men with eating disorders which left them untreated and misunderstood. That had given him no hope expecting nothing less. There is an underlying stigma of men having anorexia or bulimia which remains to be a challenge for many health professionals.

Unmasking the face of masculinity, Andre added the rarity for a man to tell other people even his family that he has eating disorder. "We just don't do it like that."

In the past, eating disorders like anorexia and bulimia were labeled as "*women's problems*" which underscored men who had the same type of condition. Unknowingly that such illness is of gender-neutral nature. In reality it doesn't choose gender, race, age, socioeconomic class. It chooses a person.

It's like Cancer. Well not quite, Mental Health America describes eating disorders as complex medical illness that have serious effects on health, productivity and relationships. It is not a phase or lifestyle choice but a bio-psycho-social condition with the highest mortality rate of any mental illness. National Eating Disorders Association (NEDA) estimates 10 million men in the United States will suffer clinically significant eating disorder at some point in their life. A silent epidemic among males with notable factors and health impact. It is not just a problem of body shaming but the inferiority that is piling up inside an individual.

Andre doesn't want to show his weakness. For him, it is more of an exposé to tell anyone about his eating disorder. And the thought that only girls or women (should) have it. He was more concerned of what other people might think while he was mostly embarrassed to tell his family. A series of flashbacks constituted an episode for him. The days when he was called the "fat boy."

As a teenager, growing up in a small town of Marshall Mississippi, Andre recalled taking diet pills to lose weight. Something he learned from reading men's sports magazine. Although he was active enough being part of the Marshall High School football team he started gaining weight which also became useful for his position as a defensive linebacker.

"I didn't want to be fat," he said.

Eating disorder long existed before the inception of the internet. It was hard especially for a young boy to find support and intervention during those times. Being on the field somewhat became a form of distraction against all the physical, emotional and social pressure he had.

He loves football.

The game helped him focused on positive things being able to look forward into winning.

On Fridays everybody was excited. On the other hand, Andre barely spoke to anyone at school that day. Averaging 11 tackles per game his mind was on one thing only.

GAME DAY.

In 1997, Andre and his teammates were playing the game of their lives against Lawrence County. The opponent needed two yards to score a touchdown, with 6-0 in the last few minutes of fourth quarter, all they had to do was defend them to win.

"How bad do you really want it?"

Andre yelled at his teammates.

"Show it to me team. Let's show 'em!"

The play was fourth and goal.

"Ready, Set, Hut, Hike…"

"…Pass Complete into the End Zone. Cougars Touchdown!"

In the locker room Andre was staring blank at the wall refusing to take off his uniform. He was catching his breath and sweat dripping off the floor. He never felt so defeated. The most important game of his senior year ended painfully. His buddies Derrick and Lucas went on to console him while convincing that he did the best he could.

Andre continued to gain weight. In addition, he suffered from depression. During those times he learned to smoke and drink. But he still was not giving up on his goal to lose weight. He pretty much told himself that this was the fight he can't afford to lose.

On the day his mother found out about the diet pills, she did not only give him a rap over the knuckles but also forced him to flush them in the toilet.

When he was fifteen, he watched his aunt grew into obesity. The casual Sunday mornings where the family gathered in church was prelude to large meals afterward. They all love to eat. She passed away at the age of 45 after suffering from a massive stroke. The same fate happened to his dear grandmother who later died due to heart failure.

There was fear of death. After seeing what happened to his family, he decided that he didn't want to fall into the same trap. He didn't want to die young and fat, he thought to himself. He felt pressured and determined to keep his weight down but because he cannot use the diet pills he had to think of a different way. It did not take a while before he figured the worst way possible to eliminate everything that he eats—by throwing up.

With no full understanding of what it was, he thought he finally found the answer as if he cracked a code or something—solving the biggest mystery in humanity. So while everybody was starving to be thin he was pigging out enjoying every meal. He did not have any worries after all the bathroom was just around the corner.

"I was looking for a quick fix to not be fat plus it didn't cost anything," Andre said. At that time it seemed to be the easiest way out. It was an idea that throwing up has given him control over his body without realizing that it was slowly taking over him and for many years to come.

In 2016, Andre had been hospitalized for five times with reasons of severe panic attack, stress and dehydration. There is nothing new to this. Somehow he is immune to the hospital environment considering it a very familiar place. He had been in-and-out of the hospital for as far as he can remember. He thinks of it somehow as a punishment from God for wasting so much food all this time. Although it could be that his body is sending him signals that it is about time for him to stop. But Andre was nowhere near to thinking of this. Fully aware of him being stubborn he made up his mind to continue the habit, because that's the only way he knows. "I'd rather be sick than be fat," Andre said.

It was a sunny afternoon, Andre was riding in the front seat with his dad. As a 15-year-old boy he did not know how to tell his father his problems, not especially a girl's problem like eating disorder. On their way to his father's barber shop, he was telling him to pack his stuff for their upcoming trip. They were going to visit his older brother in Nashville where he attended Meharry Medical College to become a doctor.

Lacking tact he muttered to himself, "I want to die." The words weren't supposed to come out but just like vomit he needed to spew.

"What did you say boy?"

He repeated himself, this time, with a loud voice and hitting his head with an open hand. "I don't like my body, I don't like the way I look...I just wanna die!!!!!"

"AHHHHH!!" Andre continuously hitting his head.

His father hit the brakes with haste causing the car to make a screeching halt. They steered to the side off the road. His father opened his door and pulled him out. He furiously stared at his son but more perturbed to know what was going on.

"What's the matter son?" his father asked. "TELL ME."

Andre kept everything to himself. He didn't want anybody, not even his family to know what he was going through. Purging deliberately became the worst habit he's ever had. His mind is filled with guilt when he feels the urge to purge. He thought, it's all in his head. He's throwing up because his mind is telling him to.

"Well, here's how it works. If you really want to know," Andre showing enthusiasm. But first, he asked me, "Did you happen to bring my cigarettes?" He was fidgeted.

As a visitor, there are certain items you cannot take into a rehabilitation facility, in his case, cigarette is one of them.

I took a bubble gum out of my purse and gave it to him.

Andre stood up and took the wrapper. He rolled it and put in his mouth as he pretended to puff away an air. Smoking calms him down, although he swore to never have smoked in front of his mother out of respect. He began to resume himself with an explanation of why he drank beer. The conversation was related to his eating disorder.

"I drink not to get drunk but to be full," Andre said. Interestingly, his argument lies on the fact that beer has calories, and so if the body needs such nutrient, he doesn't necessarily have to get it from food but instead in alcohol. If sober he would drink only flavored water, the lemon kind in particular. He also added that binge-eating is likely to happen for him when he is not drinking. "I've been around this body for a long time, trust me, I know what I'm talking about."

The idea of drinking is an unusual response to losing weight as it paints an opposite result knowing that alcohol contributes to weight gain. Even a glass of wine is similar to eating a slice of cake. But Andre pointed out that he doesn't drink hard liquor but beer alone.

People with bulimia make excuses to cover up their behavior. In a way of justifying why they do what they do. But Andre has nothing to hide, in fact, he is doing the opposite. After all, at this point, he has more self-awareness and more than willing to get help. Complications in bulimia have serious health effects and potentially life-threatening. Bulimia can lead to heart failure, kidney damage and rupture of the esophagus.

Andre deprived himself from eating processed food and although sometimes it can be tempting he rejected his own cravings, so much to it, he decided that drinking beer with four percent alcohol and 95 calories is better than eating 420 calories of hamburger or french fries.

Alternately on regular days Andre takes pride to know his way around the kitchen. He said it is one of his ironies. Perhaps one of his many talents is being able to make his favorites pasta alfredo and baked zucchini. But it isn't about what he eats, when the numb feeling starts to arise like a gridlock and pressure in his stomach—suddenly he finds the need to exude the substances.

"I can eat whatever I want to eat because I know they're going away." Andre knew that he was not going to gain weight as long as he continued with the binge-purge cycle. "I can't be fat," he insisted.

Andre recognized his eating disorder as a mental illness. The fact that he understood the urge that is coming from within and when staring at the mirror he still sees a fat person rather than his thinning body. It was becoming more visible as days passed by. The drastic weight loss followed by soreness, fatigue and muscle pain. His lethargic behavior also stopped him from working out, which used to be part of his daily routine after coming home from work. He gets off usually around five o'clock in the afternoon and spends time with his family. At seven o'clock he will be ready to go to the gym for an hour.

Apart from the sudden change in his demeanor and physical characteristics, recurrent episodes of self-induced vomiting were also evident. Andre never had used any type of laxatives to help his vomiting and perhaps he didn't need to— not when his body seems to be agreeing with it, or so he thought.

As much as Andre tried to hide it from his family and friends he revealed that it was no secret to his past relationships. Two of his previous girlfriends knew about his condition but unfortunately could not do anything to help him.

It was something they also had to bear while in a relationship with him—and hoping that one day he will get better. But that day didn't come and not even after the relationship ended.

Another irony in Andre's life is that he is a people person. However, he doesn't socialize with other people as much as he should. He would say that he is not an outgoing type of person—but he gets along with everybody. He is practically the "clown" in the family. He loves to make people laugh. A master of one-liner and silly jokes that will tickle your funny bone.

Andre finds pleasure in being able to do little things for someone without expecting anything in return—a trait he inherited from his grandmother. He recalled that a co-worker from his old job wanted to enroll in online class but didn't have enough money to buy a laptop. The next day Andre took one of his old laptops and gave it to her. He hopes that she is able to finish college.

Throughout the conversation Andre displayed a self-effacing manner—a way of telling you that he didn't want any commendation and that kindness should come naturally anyway. There is nothing Andre won't do for his family—especially for his mother. As a kid he used to watch her worked on two jobs so she would take him to his grandmother's house and picked him up later. His father was no longer in the picture and her mother could hardly make ends meet. The young Andre would ask himself what he could do to help.

When his late cousin William Alexander aka "Junior" took him to a football game in Alcorn, he had a chance to meet Steve McNair who later played in the NFL. It was a very exciting moment for Andre who once thought about going pro one day. Those ole good players who were bred from the south like Jerry Rice, Walter Payton, Brett Favre and Eli Manning who played for the University of Mississippi. Two of his contenders are the Dallas Cowboys and New Orleans Saints. He would want to see either one of them make it to the playoffs if not the Super Bowl. Entering the team locker room was better than any seats in the sideline, Andre and his cousin went to see McNair and wanted to get a picture with him but none of them had a camera. Andre took a ten-dollar bill out from his pocket and asked the player for his autograph. It was his most prized position until the day he had to sell it—in exchange for a bigger dough.

At the liquor store that is owned by his uncle Felix, a man in his 40s wearing an expensive midnight-blue suit that looked very tailored just bought a bourbon. Nonetheless he looked like somebody from out of town. Andre was showing his uncle the $10 bill with McNair's signature. He told his uncle to take a quick good look because after that he was going to put it somewhere not to be found.

"Alright nah, you're one lucky fella. Be sure to keep it safe," his uncle said. But much to Andre's excitement the man overheard him and before he could leave the store he asked, if by any chance, be willing to sell him the bill. "No sir, thank you," Andre replied. The man was very persistent with an offer that he couldn't refuse. He was willing to pay $50 for a ten-dollar bill. Andre had thought deeply about it. He looked at the bill signed by McNair one last time and accepted the man's offer.

Andre's memories come vividly with mind sharp as a tack, however, sarcastic at times for he won't take a loss at any discussion. As a student his teachers weren't able to tolerate his quick wit which somehow gave him an authority to lead a class into jeering Mr. Ford during Science. Although he confessed that his mean character was not but a defense mechanism from all his inferiorities.

Andre believed, as a kid, that he should portray himself as a menacing statue and not show any sign of weakness, because he didn't have anybody to protect him. He made a promise that he won't be a burden to his family. His mother struggled between paying the bills and raising two boys by herself. The day he saw his mother sobbing in the kitchen counter because she couldn't afford to pay the lights. Andre reached for the cabinet, inside an empty Kellogg's Corn Flakes box was that $50 bill. He gave it to her as if he knew that day would come.

Last year when Andre was hospitalized due to dehydration, following the excessive vomiting, even with the absence of food, the laboratory results may have terrified him. Apparently, his kidney and liver are thrown off-kilter. The doctor advised him to stop drinking to avoid kidney failure. It was the start of a long haul—a contemplation to live. There are only few things that will send him into a cold sweat: heights, losing a loved one and death. Andre knew he wasn't ready to die—not now when he is starting a family. It was the only thing he ever wanted to be—a father and husband. He realized he may have but one last chance.

Andre gets his nutrition from a "*banana bag*". A bag of IV fluids containing MVI or multivitamins infusion which makes the yellow substance, hence the term. It is given to patients with nutritional deficiencies. Not that he's unable to swallow, however, the fluid supply is more effective than putting food into his mouth. That way it leaves no reason for him to throw up. Aside from getting vitamins, the fluids also help alleviate the body from alcohol abuse.

The next visit. Andre showed up with a facial hair after not being able to shave for days. He hated it. He hasn't gained a pound not even close. The dietary guidelines were no help. His body didn't show any signs of progress. Andre was ready to go home. Going into rehab was his idea. He volunteered after hearing his daughter mumbled her first word "*dada*." On that day Andre broke into tears.

"I have been waiting for that day to come," he said. "I can't keep going like this."

A couple of years ago Andre couldn't care less of what the results will be. But now, as a family man, he found a purpose to head on the journey. He holds his breath when the doctor reads his diagnosis hoping that he won't find anything serious or worst to say that he has six months to live. It came to him like a pinch, an eye-opener and intimidating possibility that he might die soon. While his eating disorder has taken its toll on him, alcohol also became a problem. Andre decided to fight for his life.

Andre's decision making is not to be underestimated. At the time when he needed to choose between accepting a college football scholarship and joining the military—he weighed his options carefully. A lot of factors played on his head. But one thing was for sure—he didn't want to get any bigger. As they would require Andre to put more weight to play on defensive end, it became clearer to him which path he needed to take so he bid goodbye to being a Bulldog or Seminole. It was hard to leave the sport he truly loves but he figured there were other opportunities for him. The scout gave him two weeks to think about it and come back with an answer. Andre gave his answer right away, "Give it to somebody else. I'm done with football."

Andre and his mother took the train and went to Chicago for the first time to visit his aunt Beatrice. Being in a big city was an exhilarating experience for him. That winter Andre told himself that one day he will travel the world. "It's hard to have come from the south especially where I'm from. It's like you don't even count," he said.

Growing up he had his own share of being discriminated due to his distinctive looks which is supposedly uncommon in the Deep South. His atypical facial silhouette captures a perfect combination of more than one descent with such features of round face, high cheekbones, widened nasal tip and almond shaped eyes. On the other side he could also be mistaken for an Arabian Prince. But while his physical traits continued to change he learned to live with them.

Throughout his teenage years he rallied after all the name calling and those who dared. Although Andre was not a weakling you could easily corner in the hallway there were a couple of them who tried his patience. But quite frankly the last thing he would want was to get himself into trouble. He hated the times his mother had to show up to school because he did something wrong or that he was obviously too qualified for detention.

Perhaps a turning point in his life was during the recruitment process in the military. And when an officer told him he was "too fat to join." Although a reality to his situation that time, he didn't expect the rejection to be as hurtful and embarrassing at the same time. He would compare the same feeling as losing to a football game. More than ever before, it gave him the determination to lose weight. The idea fueled him so that he could join, as he felt he needed to. He took the challenge by doing the only regimen he knew.

The whole military physical training contributed to his weight loss. However, Andre recalled the times he had to sneak away into the woods where he found his spot and threw up. A man in his fatigue uniform hid behind the trees while he purged, that's how he remembered himself.

Andre was stationed in Germany.

It started as a call of duty but he ended up embracing the culture. He was fascinated with it that he decided to stay after his assignment. For a country boy who haven't been to many places, Bamberg was a whole different world. Initially he became one of the tourists strolling around the cobbled lanes and narrow medieval streets in town. But aside from the experience of beautiful sceneries and architectural masterpieces he also wanted to be able to communicate with the people.

In reality, he needed to learn the German language in order for him to get by. He thought of starting a new life with no intention of returning to the United States. He wanted to live there.

"I didn't want to go back," Andre said. "*Es war völlig anders und sie waren so freundlich Menschen.*"

It means "It was totally different and they were such friendly people." Andre speaks German fluently. He bears all of his experiences with that German flag tattooed on his right arm.

In the evenings, after getting off work from the factory he would ride the bus from his place to go to Sprachschule für Deutsch als Fremdsprache in Erlangen. Where he went to learn German as a foreign language. It didn't come as a requirement but he felt compelled to adapt their ways and in order to do so he needed to become one of them, as Andre would say. What he learned from high school also became useful. At that time, Andre picked to learn German while others took Spanish class. He first learned to say "*Guten Morgen*" which means Good Morning.

Despite the change of environment and lifestyle he continued to suffer from eating disorder. He tried to get help from different specialists in Berlin. However, he was referred to a mental institution which he refused to go. Andre didn't want to live his life with worries and so he considered it no luck.

In 2010, Andre decided to go back to the United States. It was a difficult decision but he thought of being with his family. For almost ten years he spoke a different language living in contrast to everything he knew of. At first it became a problem, for he didn't know where to start. Everything is different. Everything has changed. The southern customs somehow appeared unfamiliar to him. He took a step back from living abroad to coming home to Mississippi. He was willing to give an exemption. But he did it to look after his old mother.

The trunk slowly popped open. He moved inconspicuously to step out and run for the door. He hopped into the car and breathed a sigh of relief. It was early in the morning and the sun was strikingly yellow. Andre had slept in the trunk overnight. It happened for the second time because he was too drunk to drive. There were no taxis in downtown Jackson, not especially at midnight.

"I didn't want anybody to see me drunk," Andre said.

He got in trouble last time he slept in his car and parked across the Waffle House at McDowell Road. The police came and approached him after the waitress called in to report a suspicious man. They let him go after identifying himself. But he learned that he can no longer sleep in the car, not to mention it being in one of the most dangerous areas in Jackson. The capital city ranked No. 6 on cities with the highest murder rates out of Top 30 based on the 2015 FBI Uniform Crime Reporting Program. But Andre who used to work for the Artillery Unit in the Army could not be bothered. "It would be hard to sneak up on me," he said. Andre didn't want to sound political so he kept his other comments to himself.

While struggling to find a job he had to live with his mother because he couldn't afford to pay for an apartment. He didn't like the idea but he had to swallow his pride. Andre doesn't like asking people for help not even from his family.

"I'm a giver not a taker," he said.

Andre would spend a lot of his time at his favorite place— the Lake Eleanor. He likes to watch the water while listening to the sound of silence that accompanies the breathtaking view. A place where he would go to think. There must be a way to fight against it, he thought. He took his condition as a challenge.

He did—as he would stop throwing up for a few months. Andre thought that was the end of it but he was wrong.

He would throw up four times in a day. The forceful discharge of his stomach was unbearable. He was weak and tired. He realized that he needed help. His condition has become a hurdle to his life and work.

Andre used to tell his coworkers that he was going on a vacation, when in fact, he was getting himself admitted to the hospital. The binge-purge cycle worsened.

Andre told himself to stop.

"I kept saying STOP. Just stop," he said. But it wasn't that easy.

Soon he was dependent on medication. His doctor prescribed him with some folic and multivitamins to give nutrients to his body. He also took a sedative called lorazepam for a week to reduce the symptoms of alcohol withdrawal when he decided to stop drinking. He experienced all sorts of discomfort which included hand tremors and difficulty in breathing.

"I am not taking those pills again. Never," Andre said.

Mixing lorazepam with other substances can be extremely dangerous. On the other hand, Andre was drinking more than six bottles a day while taking the medication. It was the worst idea.

Andre almost had an overdose.

His body was paralyzed and he couldn't move. He was lucky enough to have high tolerance with such chemicals—or he could've died.

It was hard to convince him not to throw up. Andre's tough personality made it harder for people around him to help, even his mother, who wasn't too happy to discover the condition of her son. Although he didn't want to upset her—it was time for the family to know.

"Unbelievable."

"What were you thinking huh?"

His brother went to see him at the hospital. Andre doesn't trust anybody but his family. It's hard to talk him out of something once he made up his mind.

"I didn't know man. I'm sorry," Andre said.

The man who entered the room looked exactly like him.

Dr. Jesse Spencer.

Everybody knows him especially the people from Metro Jackson. He made his hometown proud when he was awarded "*Healthcare Visionary*" by the Jackson Free Press for four consecutive years since 2014. He was also selected as one of the Top 40 Under 40 business leaders in 2012 by the Mississippi Business Journal. A primary care physician who also happens to be his big brother.

A popular face in media being a regular contributing medical expert for the local television news stations. In 2009, Dr. Spencer was featured as an expert physician for the Black Entertainment Television (BET) Network Special, "Jackson vs Food." He also appeared on NBC Nightly News which is hosted by Lester Holt.

"You could've died. You know that right," he said.

"Why are you doing this to yourself bro? You have a beautiful family. A great job. I mean, you are living the life. So what's the problem?" There was a little tension in his voice.

"Because I'm sick man, that's why," Andre replied

"I don't want this. Do you think I like going to the hospital every week? Shit! I didn't choose this. I'm tired."

Andre was teary-eyed. LOOK AT ME!!

"..Help me…help me."

Jesse was filled with remorse as he looked at his brother.

The two brothers grew up together. Although they were separated in time pursuing different paths in life. They remain very close.

Jesse remembered that day he had to punch somebody in the face after he caught some kids picking on his little brother while calling him fat. He was 14-years-old then but strong enough to shove the boy in the ground. He told his brother to get tough.

Jesse would also pick his own brother when they were young. That time when he poured the cereal into the sink because he didn't want him to be fat.

He said, "You can't eat that, you're already fat." He recalled his words.

Somehow that memory got stuck in Andre's head as he would remind himself one of the reasons why he didn't want to be fat was because his brother told him not to. And all he wanted was to become just like him.

He wanted to be accepted.

Although with such different personalities the two brothers excelled in so many things.

Jesse looked out for him until he had to leave to go to college.

"I'm sorry I wasn't there," Jesse said. "I didn't mean to come at you like this but you scared the hell out of me. You're my brother and mom is worried sick about you."

"You have to get better bro," he added.

Andre's physician came into the room.

"How's everything going? I heard the famous Dr. Spencer is in the building so I thought I'd pay my respects," said Dr. McNeese. It was his first time meeting the two brothers and he was rather excited.

"No sir, don't say that. I'm just a regular doctor at your service," Jesse turned red-face.

"Alright, alright, alright."

Dr. McNeese flipped through his chart. He placed the head of the stethoscope on Andre's chest.

His heart sounded lub-dub..lub-dub..lub-dub.

Jesse was anxious as he asked, "What do we have doc?"

He read out loud, "His chemistry panel was normal. His MCV or size of red blood cells was somewhat elevated. His liver panel including AST and ALT was actually all normal today."

"You'll be fine son," said the doctor.

He also added that Andre could be discharged that same day.

While driving their way home Andre saw a billboard sign just past Northside Drive. It was his brother's face on the ad.

He gave it a smirk.

"What's wrong?" Jesse asked.

"Nothing. I just find it funny sometimes," Andre replied. "These people don't know the story. They're probably thinking that we had it good. They think they know you as the pretty doctor driving that 2016 Porsche 911, that's right. As for me, it surprises them to find out that I'm your brother."

"I guess it will be hard for me to keep up with you man," Andre added.

"Don't ever feel that way. You're smarter and stronger than me," Jesse said. He recounted that it was never easy. And that he could've stayed in California after his residency, but he chose to come back for his family. "Do you remember what grandmother used to tell us? She'd tell you to be yourself, "be Andre," and that's all that matters bro."

As if it was yesterday one of them would go to the store carrying a bag of loose change and pour into the coin-cashing machine. It answered to an old tale that any bill is better than a quarter.

They reflected on how the tables have turned for them.

"Do you think it would have been different if he didn't leave us?" Andre asked.

They both went quiet.

It occurred to me that after eating he would sneak his way to the bathroom. I could hear the water running, at first, I thought he would gurgle and rinse his mouth. It was until later that I realized I should have paid more attention to look further than what was obvious.

That day I asked him, "Baby did you throw up?"

One of the many times I have asked the same question.

He shook his head and said, "Ah-ah. Why?"

I asked again, "Are you sure?"

He said, "No, I didn't throw up."

And even with his incessant denial I could see he was hiding something from me.

After all, I am confident enough to know my husband that well.

But I guess I also respected his own sense of privacy. I wanted to wait until he was ready to tell me. I began to fret, on each passing day, not knowing what was going on. But perhaps deep inside I was more than terrified to hear the words come out from his mouth.

There were many scenarios that would play in my head. What if he had brain tumor that was spreading fast like a time bomb waiting to explode? Or that one day his heart stopped pumping blood that resulted to his collapse? What if he had ALS?

All of my speculations have put me in the most pessimistic way possible.

The first time he took me to Lake Eleanor I was stunned by its beauty. I didn't come from Mississippi so I'm not familiar with its natural landscape. This place is quite a surprise to me. The water is calm. He was right—it does give you that sense of tranquility.

When we found out that we were having a girl the joy was inexplicable.

As I look at our daughter I feel blessed. She makes me the happiest person in the world.

I rolled the camera and took a video of him holding Emma.

"Hey baby, look at the camera. Look at the camera. It's mommy."

"Look at the camera Emma," he said.

She gave us a smile. Her face resembles her father. This was exactly how I imagined it. Perhaps I was overthinking. Maybe it's nothing serious. But before I could confront him or his sickness, he told me.

Andre has bulimia.

He admitted that he had been throwing up for a long time. It wasn't easy for him to tell but he didn't want to lie to me anymore. I was dazed by his revelations.

He continued to fill me with the story of how it all started.

Although I should be relieved that it was not cancer, I felt more terrified of the situation.

I fear for him. I didn't know what to say except I told him, "I love you. I'm here for you."

I started reading about eating disorders. All of them pointed out to death. But no, I don't want to think of that.

Another day, I watched him put on his clothes as he would go to work. They don't fit the same. He adjusted his belt but there was no more left to cinch. At first, he asked me to get a knife so he could make another hole, but he found a pair of scissors in one of our drawers which he used instead.

Then he said, "I'm gone baby. Let me see if I could make us a few more dollars."

He kissed me goodbye.

Days. Weeks. Months.

June. July. August.

In September, Andre saw that his vomiting had pushed to a greater degree and that if he didn't stop he could die. While holding hands he said to me, "If you don't see me again, please don't forget about me." I said "No, we're not going there."

I could not have prepared myself for what happened. And only if I could take some of his pain I would have done it already. Andre never failed to show his love for me and our daughter. In his own little ways and the simplest things that touched my heart. He is my inspiration, my best friend, my gift. Needless to say, he is my one true love.

He gave me a smile and said, "Tell me something good."

At that point fear and doubt circled my head. I didn't want to cry because despite of it all we both found ourselves closer and hopeful together. We see to it to be thankful for what we have to share, yet, the best that has ever happened to us, our daughter. There were so many things I would want to say but I guess I'd rather keep them with me. Like good memories, they stay with me.

I read him those lines from that card I made for his birthday. It goes.

"Along the way, though, we laugh and love
and learn so much about ourselves and each

other. And even when we're not really sure
exactly where it is we'll end up, we always
know that we'll arrive the same way we set out."
And he said "Thank You."

The next day we went to the lake as he requested.

He looked at the view for minutes. The breeze was somehow our companion. He threw a stone across the water as it bounced off the surface. He looked calmed.

He reached for my hand. We stood in front of the beauty and awe of the sunset. Looking ahead.

It was our last day together before he left to get his residential treatment. His decision of getting help was a big step on his road to recovery. Andre took his challenge and promised to get better.

The Newcomer

IF IT WASN'T FOR HIM I wouldn't feel this kind of guilt again. The kind that will stomp you harder than you might think. I can only care for a few people and little things because I have taught myself to be less affected about their potential causes.

For the last three years I have convinced myself that I'm in a right direction. As I would imagine I see myself working in an office. I thought about it before, I'm going to be a shrink. That's right, I like the idea of just sitting in a chair while listening to people—their frustrations in life.

I would simply say "*How do you feel about that?*" and then I'm done for the day. Perhaps it can get a little overwhelming but I've had a good training.

In case you're wondering I'm good at listening if someone has a problem. I'm a good listener if I could put it that way. Since I'm taking this up in college I thought there's no other way of doing it. It's a full proof plan I said to myself.

So basically, it is my goal to be able to understand people. I want to know why they do what they do. Why we do what we do? I'm always wondering what's going on inside their head. I don't read minds. That thing leaves me out in curiosity. It keeps me interested.

Of course, I don't blame that most people think when you're a psychologist you ought to be able to read minds, I just don't think it's always the case. Everybody lies, everybody cheats. So even if you read their minds and tell them they're wrong they still do it anyway.

I remember once telling Alex, a friend of mine, to stop chatting with this guy she met online. A fifty-four-year-old Danish who claims to be a divorce businessman looking for a serious relationship. Seriously, I mean, do you really think the person whom you are going to share your life with can be found in some random website asking for your card number. I don't think so. Alex told me she was just using him for extra money she's been saving to go on a European trip with her boyfriend and other friends. I didn't approve but she was pretty insistent and quite proud of how much she's already got. That should be enough to go around shopping in Paris she exclaimed. Boy she has some talent I thought. Well she's also smart although you wouldn't think of that when you first see her. A brunette with perfect locks and golden skin. She smiles and waves to everyone at school as if she knows them but really she just likes the attention. Well she is pretty popular. That is so typical if you know what I mean. But there was a time she showed an unexpected wit and helped me out with some Humanities assignment, and I did get a good grade on that. Anyway, sooner or later her boyfriend Matt found out when he went to her house for a visit. He always comes whenever her parents are out of town. Alex was just getting ready to wear her costume probably to give that old fella a virtual lap dance and all when Matt arrived in her room. I could have told you the whole story but that would be unethical. Yes, I'm practicing my core starting with this one. So, it didn't work with them as Matt broke up with Alex. She was left devastated that she'd call me up 3:00 o'clock in the morning sobbing. Who does that? But I'm being a friend so I'd comfort her in any way I can. That's what I do. But really now that all her European dream tour has perished in an instant I'd love to tell her "I told you so," but that's too cliché so I probably won't.

I'm not giving her a relationship advice anytime soon. It somehow made me realized that I'm not going to be a psychotherapist for immature couples unable to maintain their sanity together.

I hate to admit but I only had one relationship and it ended pretty badly so I don't think I'm the best person to ask when it comes to such things. In fact, I try to distance myself from those topics in as much as possible. Relationships and Politics: two things I can't stand in this world. That could become one of my weaknesses in the future should I choose to pursue this so-called career.

And there's Jonathan, well this guy is unpredictable. I can't remember when we became friends in the first place. I used to not like him. I don't know he seemed a little off to me back then, that's all. But that was before I have gotten to know him better. They call him "Jonathan Wilbert", "Jonathan Arms", "Big J"..basically all the pet names dubbed for him by the boys R boys crew. I don't think he's a jerk, although sometimes he kinda is. But he's a guy so what do you expect. But he's not like them you know, those guys who think of themselves as Masters of the Universe. He is a bit different. I know he is, because he's my friend and it only means he's a good person, that's all. Now going back, Jonathan has been seeing a therapist lately. This was after he found a body of a freshman student who was supposed to join the football team. The boy committed suicide. He did it in the auditorium. It was one of the gloomiest days in campus. Until now it remains a mystery why that poor guy ended his life. We all know this world can be cruel sometimes, *But Still!* So whenever Jonathan doesn't feel like talking to his official shrink he'll show up to my door steps. I like having simple conversations with him. His jokes bleed dry but they make me laugh. They can turn out to be funny. Also, I haven't met a guy who reads Nicholas Sparks. Gasp. The thing is I don't even read those kinds of books and he does so somehow it manages to make me feel a little incompetent. No actually, it makes me feel ineffectual which is unacceptable.

Mr. Alcott our Biology professor once told us that if we want to make it we should learn to be grateful first before we demand something out of this life. I thought it meant something. That's the thing about older people they'd love to give us the proverbs. Sometimes they don't really say it to our face and want us to find the answer ourselves. They think that's how we learn. They let us wander inside a jungle. I'm not even sure if they try to find us after. They tell us things that are full of crap. If I want to be inspired by anything or anyone I'd probably just sit myself at home, get some crackers and watch a documentary about children in Africa, dying from hunger. But that would be too impulsive as I'm such an easy crier so I'd reserve that idea.

But really, if there's one thing I should be thankful for in this world, that's my Aunt Judith. She's the only family I have now and I owe it everything to her. She could be a little dull, hot tempered, quite a traditionalist but she raised me all by herself so I chose not to complain. She is a retired Science teacher. She used to teach in high school at William Boroughs, but after being hospitalized many times she was advised to take a rest indefinitely. I bet those bastards made her sick that's why. Good old boys can be such tools. They've done a great job. They really did. I heard somewhere that another teacher in that school suffered from laryngitis because she kept on yelling in her class. That was screwed up. I ended at my Aunt Judith's care after my mom died. She is not a relative but I call her Aunt anyway.

I like knowing these things, being with these people and having a suppose career plan for the future. I thought I have them figured out. I thought I was in a right direction. But right now I found myself pacing on the streets of Hoboken to dither every stranger asking them if they've seen a kid.

Me: "Excuse me, have you seen this kid?"

Stranger: "No."

Me: "Have you seen this kid?"

Stranger: "Umm, No. Sorry."

Me: "Have you seen this kid?"

Stranger: *stares blankly*

As I show them a picture of me and this kid on my phone I'm starting to feel numbness inside me. In everytime these people would answer No. I want to smother them for saying that word and just move on. I don't blame them. I don't have the right. And it's not their fault. It's my fault. The night is my only companion in this chase of uncertainty. This heart is beating unusual becoming heavy, in my mind, God I refuse to pass out. I'm searching every corner with no intention of stopping until I find him.

Shit!

(Whispers) Where are you?

WHERE ARE YOU?-----
-------RYAN!

TWO MONTHS AGO

Early this summer Alex decided to retire from being an online companion to be a hippie loafer, well at least nearly becoming. This, I would like to believe is a post-breakup stage after her boyfriend dumped her which was her fault anyway. I refuse to take an influence from her, neither do I need to be influenced with such things by anyone.

"C'mon guys it's so freaking late! And you, I can't believe you drove us when you're drunk. You should be arrested."

"Sssshhh, We know." (Laughing) ensue.

"Well, it's still…just…12:30----- IN THE MORNING."

"Urggg, just let me out of the car already and go. Alex, please SMS me when you get home. I want to know if you're still alive by then. PLEASE!"

"YES sir! (Laughs—burps)."

The car screeched its way after I let myself out. I know this is not a good behavior but it happens sometimes. I, for one, am a responsible drinker. I know my limitations and so I don't compromise but there are just times these people are so out of control and seemingly they can somehow influence you in a manner you wouldn't know behind your neck. Unfortunately, that's what happened to me in this case. So, I fear that in this crack of dawn I'd find myself facing a trial in front of my Aunt's dining table. I thought about it, thus, I'm on guard with precautionary details to suffice her rather scientific argument. But let's face it, the ship for a simple-group-study-for-an-upcoming-Biology-Mastery-Test has already sailed. I can even smell the alcohol inside me. Shit! What were those people drinking? I feel like I'm wearing an extra helmet that my head feels so heavy and the surrounding starts to spin. I have slumber party written all over me. Only I'm not wearing pajamas. I spray some perfume in my mouth, fix my top and two slaps on my right cheek to wake me. I maintain composure as I slowly twist the knob. I entered the house successfully. I'm ready for my Aunt's sermon as I've pictured her impatiently waiting in the sofa or at the dining table, but she's not there. For a moment I feel so relieved. I would hurry to my room before she'd notice then the phone rang, I stopped. I mean, who would have called in this hour and I hope it's not the police who caught my abandoned companions DUI. The phone rang again and I picked up.

"Oh Thank God, Hello, this is Sally from St. Joseph Medical Center…"

I surely don't know any Sally from that hospital but I can tell she was so relieved to be able to speak to me. But I still wonder why I am getting this call at this point of hour.

"We were trying to reach your cell but it kept on sending us to voice mail until we weren't able to reach you at all. I'm just calling to inform you that Ms. Judith has been admitted around 2:45PM today she came in with chest pain. You're on her immediate contact list so we've been trying to call you. Are you her daughter?"------

I still have that numbness inside as I try to assemble those words I've just heard. I didn't have the slightest idea that my aunt was in the hospital the whole time I passed out in a sloppy drinking session. What happened to her? Is she okay? Is she gonna live? All these questions started popping out of my brain, but I have no time for that. I went straight to the hospital and asked the first attendant at the Information.

———

Today is Aunt Judith's birthday, just like every year she doesn't want any preparations. But I thought this year should be different, considering that she'll be celebrating it in that hollowed private room, so I rushed in ordering her favorite cake. She is no longer allowed to eat anything sweet but I'm going to spare her on this particular occasion. And really, NOT eating anything sweet is like being deprived from fresh air. I could have baked a simple orange cake with some icing and nips on top but I thought that wouldn't be age appropriate so I decided to go to Torya's Sweet Box. They have the wildest-sweetest-sweets of cakes in the entire New Jersey. I will pledge on that with great sincerity in unbiased way. Really top notch. I entered the shop and saw Carol quite busy near the counter. I give her a nod as she sees me heading towards her direction.

"Hi, I'm picking up an order."

"Oh, hello dear, I haven't seen you in a while. How you been? I'm sorry to hear about Judith. How is she doing?

"She is doing well. It was one of her symptoms. So, she needed to stay there for a few days for some tests and observation."

"Ahh, I hate it when they do those things. It's not pleasant." She said.

"Well, it's her birthday today. I ordered a Decadent."

"Ahh, yes, you have. Now, would you like some dedication to be put on top? We can make it Italic."

I havven't really thought about any dedication. But this is the first time I'm buying her a cake so maybe it's only right.

"Well…um, just Happy Birthday! Love Eden" I said.

"…and no flowery decoration or anything."

"Well, maybe we'll do that part for you."

You see I'm not really good in dedications. I have no use for them so I don't practice.

Besides if you buy gifts you can always get a card with pre-made greetings.

Carol is the owner and she's hands on with her business. She comes in almost everyday so she manages to get to know people in this area. After her husband died she has all more reason to get her hands full. I know she's of Portuguese descent. Her family moved here when she was thirteen so that rustic little accent is just lovely.

This neighborhood is a little too compressed, if you ask me. Like anywhere else, people here just come and go, but you'd know if someone is new.

I was born in San Francisco, I lived there until I was six before my parents got divorced so me and my mom went East.

The day that we came here was a blur, at least that's how I want to remember it.

———

This pastry shop was the first place we found since my mom also had a weakness for sweets. I'd come here oftentimes since I was in Junior High. Okay, so I have a soft spot for their éclairs. But if you've tried it yourself you'd know why.

The shop is now expanded to accommodate more customers and those who enjoy early breakfast in sidewalks. I know I do. As I'm waiting for that cake to be ready, I can't help but notice this middle-aged guy outside while he sips his cup of coffee. He's reading a book entitled "*White Cliffs And Such*," which I haven't heard of. I thought maybe this guy is a shrink. He could be Jonathan's shrink for all I know. I mean, this town is pretty boxed out so you can imagine the possibilities. His dark hair is obviously dyed so I'd take he used to be a blond. His pale white long-sleeves are tucked in his faded jeans. He pleats a page of that book and sets it aside on the table to have another sip, then lights a cigarette. He looks around while people are passing by as if he's familiarizing each one of them. He has a sharp look on his face.

"Alright, it's all good now. We made it extra special for her."

"Thanks."

"And oh, here's a little something for you. I know just how much you love them."

"ECLAIRS"

Carol slips a little giveaway for me and something that I can't resist.

"Thank you very much" I said.

"Tell your Aunt Judith Happy Birthday for me, will you? And I may have time to visit her tomorrow."

"I sure will."

"Oh, by the way, how's your new neighbor?

"What neighbor?"

"You have a new neighbor, right? Haven't you met them yet?"

I haven't really figured out which neighbor she's talking about because I don't roam door-to-door to get to know people. Although I know quite a few people in our block. I just don't know which neighbor she's talking about this time. And I'm already ardent to indulge myself with these little sweets.

"Oh that, well they're very *neighboree*. Very friendly" I said.

"Good. We need more people like that in this town" she said.

Before leaving the shop I thought of asking her if she happens to know the man outside.

"No. I don't recognize him dear. Why?"

"Nothing."

"I thought this café is a smoke-free environment."

"Well, he's technically outside. Besides, he could be a tourist." She responded.

I didn't want to bother her with my typical judgments so I pretended to agree.

"Right. Well thank you again. I'll come by maybe next week."

Where The Light Meets

PART I
RIDING THE WAVES

"She made broken look beautiful and strong look invincible. She walked with the universe on her shoulders and made it look like pair of wings."

THERE IS A SUDDEN RUSH in the wind and you can feel its coldness. Beneath the skies you see a gloomy face in front of this painful recollection. A memory that should've been gone long ago to better not reminisce everything in the past. A wilderness maybe of what used to be. There was once a thought. A small town in Guernica is the place she'd rather be. An irony to her emotions but the only way she recalls. In a way she didn't want to vanish them all. She's empty. She's holding onto it—a grasp of hope. Years have passed but it seemed like it happened yesterday. The unwillingness to see their faces again. This longing is forever although she knows one day she'll be there. That happy place they've once talked about. Her face is pale with no emotions showing outside. Emilia just moved into this town. Nobody knows her except the people from that place she goes every morning, probably the way she starts her day. For those who didn't know she used to be a girl who looked up the sky with innocence. One summer, the shadow of darkness cast over her. She was devastated. And though she tries to go on, her soul is buried somewhere. In that exact same place where they were. The night crawls upon her as she sits by the window. She can see the sky. She raises her arm as if she's touching it. Where the clouds and stars meet. They gather around in space. They glide with each other, for they are too in a journey. The light that we see now. It's heaven. A representation of hope and love. A bridge of one place to another. The ones who wonder are those who travel. They don't see time, nor do they pay attention to it. They carry on. People who have been through places are more experienced and exposed. They've met and seen different faces and probably fell in love too. Oh, love. That's exactly the word Emilia needs. For a long time she can't feel it. She doesn't see it or perhaps she refused to.

Rewind—no more pain. Live with no memory. What about the ones you love? Exactly the reason why. For they are no longer there. The premature deaths of her parents became a customary trauma for her inevitable self-pity. As not all orphans do well thereafter. She doesn't speak to anyone. She learned to shut it off. Believing that by doing this she won't feel the pain. She wouldn't be bothered by sadness.

As she walks in the downtown area, at least, there's one thing left for her to do. She goes to a facility where old people go. She feels safe there and somehow connected. Emilia thought to herself if she'd live long enough with such punishment, this is where she would go. There's something about being in that place that comforts her. It calms her in a way when she's around them. The ones who've already fought life and somehow at the verge. She's walking toward a man.

"Oh, it's you. I thought I wouldn't be seeing you again." A seventy-two-year-old man named Miguel is sitting in a wheelchair. She greets him.

"How are you today?"

"Ugh, I've had bad days. If that makes this one better."

"I was wondering if I could spend sometime with you today, if that's okay with you." Emilia asked.

They talked for about an hour before the nurse came. It's dinner time and everybody is headed to the dining hall.

"Well it's been a pleasure talking to you Carol, but I have to go with this young lady now."

Emilia gave him a smile. She didn't mind that he called her a different name. He does that all the time. Although she hopes he remembers her one day. But whoever *Carol* is—she's a lucky woman.

"I will see you again next time."

A true wonder of life.

We are born, then we are a child. We are young, then we are old.

We live and we die. The stages we go through in life are in cycle. In case you didn't notice we are coming around in a circle. Existing is not enough. We must live. Life is too short for that. No guarantee. No promises. But don't be reckless because you only have but one chance to do it right. Emilia thinks of herself as a passenger of life these days. She doesn't really know where it's headed. But she couldn't care any less.

She is only waiting. And this is not how she imagined it. She feels the cold wind again.

"Emilia," said a voice that sounded familiar to her.

Someone is calling her name. She looked around to find no one else. Her skin crawled with shivers. She swore she's heard of that voice before. In her mind maybe it's only an illusion, an outcome of her exhaustion. Emilia went to several places and found nothing. It didn't catch her attention. Not quite. If today was your last day. What would you do? A question not for her but for everyone out there. We are surrounded by so many things. But what is more important? If you've seen quite enough you know it's not the material things. They perish and with no value. And yes, it's true. They say that. We don't take anything with us when it's time for us to go.

Tick! Tock!

We all have time. But we use it differently. We compromise and sometimes abide. Anything goes these days. But not for a while. It can't keep going like this. And like a bursting pipe it will happen soon enough. When reality hits and it will hit us hard. Especially the ones who are not prepared. This is War. It is coming. If you don't see it then you are naïve, in your sleep. There's cause and effect in what you do. Enjoy this little time we share for now. It is only for a moment. A time wasted is a time not spent. It's almost the same. Do a thing that makes you happy. That limelight is temporary. Go to places and discover new things.

She remembers them. Of when they were around. The happiest memories and sad ones. There are echoes in the background. Choose your own sound. They are reflections of your thoughts. The bright ones are loud. They are optimistic for what's to come. While others are cautious and afraid. They don't bet in life for they don't want to lose. They pick their battles and this one is not for them. They don't want to lose.

What you see is a mirror of what's happening. But it contains the evolution of time. Of People. Present. Future. They're all changing. What was once there is now a memory.

A thought perhaps. It is not that easy nor simple. This is unlike what they think. Because the good ones are gone. Too early to be gone. If you sing me a lullaby I wouldn't faint. I wouldn't be asleep. I will be counting days. Yes, I am hopeful for tomorrow.

She paused herself for a minute and thought of the Sunday brunch—where they used to go. At Larson Street, that's where their favorite restaurant is. Accompany her as she passes through the same sidewalks. She sees the same ole people where they sat and nod at her. She's overwhelmed and shaking in every pace, but she just wants to see him again. And only through the smoke he'll appear in front of her. His face she still remembers. His smile and his voice. That's right. The exact same voice she heard the other day. She should've known. It was him. Slowly his shadow is disappearing as she tries to reach for his hand, he's gone. She heard the whistle of her tea pot. She let the curtains down.

Of trees and branches. We see them everywhere and in our own backyard. They glide and hold on strong. But dependent to its soil. When it's thirsty, it needs water. Where there's too much light, it needs a shade. There grow all the passages of those who are in joy and pain. They go together one and the same. It is not a flock. At least not for all. Sometimes they go individually and soon enough they will learn. It is a discovery of oneself. Whether you get lost or whatnot you'll soon find your way. The distance is only a matter of time. But keep moving until you get there. It is easier to forget than remember. If only you can choose the memories you've had. But they are all part of you. They consist. If you can eliminate the ones you didn't like. Something you cannot control. The only difference lies on the choices we make. A challenge we must take amidst all the temptations on the way.

Emilia let the days passed. Thinking there will always be tomorrow. Although with pure intentions and fueled ambition she was in the unknown of what was to happen. There's no telling. The future doesn't need your permission. It's continuous. It's fast and changing. Day and night. It comes and it goes. The smallest things in life—they count. For what you don't see is not there. It is everywhere. When the past is chasing you, be brave. Things you need to remember. A reminder of what used to be. Given that you have the power to change the course of where you are headed. Where do you go? For years and years, she asked herself. Questions that she wanted answers seemed unknown. She learned for a while what she needed to. But it's not enough. Her dreams are made of the deconstruction of what she's been keeping in a long time. She's a wanderer. Allowing new ideas to enter. She's vulnerable. She's running away from her dreams. They haunt her. It's a different picture of what she would like. As if somebody is pulling the strings off against her. She's both strong and fragile. She continues to hold on.

Emilia has been through all the sessions. She had different prescription. Her past is rooted in the deepest part of her wounds. When she closes her eyes, she'd like to escape.

Memories are memories.

But don't forget reality.

Good fortune. Oh, how great!

The wonders we experience. They are elements. Of us. Of nature. Don't tire yourself with the nonsense. Some trees don't bear a fruit but still they stand. Hope is powerful. Let it be yours.

She used to be graceful. The days have gone and nothing's changed. Everything looks the same. The clouds aren't moving. She isn't either. She misses her mother and the way she sang her lullaby. Why it happened? She was young and innocent. She didn't know any better. Like a puzzle she couldn't put the pieces together. A picture of her parents she kept since she was a child. She didn't have enough time to spend. And it happened again.

Her parents were good people. The good kind. The only thing she likes from her memory and if she could pick one. She used to be grateful for everything and all things that surround her. She didn't know any better.

Don't carry the things you can't take with you. There are greater treasures on the way. They are more valuable. It doesn't say a happy ending but always believe there is. Love is powerful. Love is relentless.

When you hope for something bigger. You must be willing to take what is given. Take the risk. It all depends.

She learned to swim in the depths of her grief. For she knew then what she had to do. She promised them. She will remember. It made her tough. She didn't fear. She slowly understood. But sorrow was a mean enemy. She cries in her sleep for years. All things that don't mean anything to her. She was like a prisoner of her own. She dreamt of her parents and for a moment she was safe. She got up and nobody was there. She's used to being alone.

This night is quiet. When she thinks of it despite of hurt, and all other things. If things were different. How life would have turned out? All the things that she had learned. Will they matter? The way they taught her. They will always be in her heart.

Later, she sees herself in a different picture. A privilege to see through the lens of another person's life. She enjoys that part. Taking photos. In every click. She becomes one of them in that instant. She admires the beauty of nature. She finds her peace in the sound of the wind.

When the only escape sometimes is reality. What do you fear? Look up and see a different side. It's not perfect. The world is beautiful but it's not perfect. So are the people you see. There's no happiness without remembering sorrow. To have an open mind is to live. Soon enough you will learn to navigate. Let no murmurs be a discouragement. Let go of sadness.

Emilia has grown to fight the odds. She battles her nightmares and fears. The undesirable memories, she learned to turn them around. Looking at the other side of the picture. Chasing the past is like chasing waves.

It was not but an ordinary night. A loud siren spread in the corners and every inch of the town. It was dark and stormy. The patrol car and ambulance were parked on the side of the highway.

They rang an accident.

A sweeping melody to match an event. Foggy dark clouds in the sky. You don't see anybody. Not one walking in the alley. A tension to this tragedy. Although it's almost too late but it's necessary. The ones who should know. About what happened.

He didn't get lost in the woods but in the middle of that road when the breaks fooled him. He didn't see it coming.

The way you see things is not the way it should be. It's not the same thing.

Align the stars if you can, if you will. But they'll always go back to their forms and be scattered in space. From where they were born.

The wind blew and sent the message. Unfortunate one. The sad truth. However, it is. When it comes and it goes. It's only for a little while but they don't stay. They are going toward different paths. Still shaking from the news. She cried for herself. The man she loves is gone. Been to different places with nothing else but deceit. It blinds you sometimes. Search for truth. Not that easy. And when you found one. Allow yourself to experience both ends and perhaps you'll find out why. But when you're blinded, you'll make the stops. You are not contended. The longing continues. Whenever she remembers him, she'll try to smile. And when she feels the guilt. It cuts down her imagination. In the hopes of finding herself. Of starting over. She thought about it a lot of times. It takes courage to accept the fact. While doing so there's another arrow thrown at you. So you were told, do what you have to.

- The air breathes slow. It needs a rest.

- Exhausted from the nightmares.

Emilia lost her man. It was abrupt. They were paired as one. He filled her when she was hollow. She was troubled with no direction. All the rambling thoughts in her head, they must be gone. Pause for a moment. Then reconnect herself.

—

She is a photographer.

She collects memories and put them into picture. A present for those who've asked. Emilia didn't want to share her art. They are not for sale. Although people from the old town heard about her, it was hard for them to take a glimpse. The ones who have seen it, probably dug deep enough to find the collection she's never shown to anyone before. It was in her photos that she found companionship. She was intrigued and enlightened at the same time. It gave her a thrill and sense of pleasure. She found something she was proud of. She is fond of the portraits. They speak to her. And to the amusement of Albert after he finally witnessed such magnificent pieces, an ecstatic feeling that was almost grateful. He wanted to convince her to share some of the images. She disagreed. With no intention of doing so. They argued for a moment. Raising voices at each other while ruled with their emotions. Although it didn't take long before he wrapped her around his arms. An apologetic gesture to make her feel safe again. Then she was calmed. Troubled feelings collide but at that time only, love is greater than any other object.

A companion to where she goes. Unwillingly she assembles herself to face the present time. All together pain makes it harder for her. The weight that has become a burden.

When she closes her eyes, she'll see their faces. Her parents were the best part of her memory. The only thing that she would like to keep. She long for the love of family. The one she lost. The feelings kept in the dark. Emilia learned the hardest part. Where at night she speaks to their souls, a vow she made to Albert, she too honors. A purpose must be found. Understand things not for what they are. Withstand the waves that are coming behind. Whether it's a burden or a curse, she takes it. Choice is not given sometimes. What you allow is what you have. They're passing through time. Don't hold 'em, learn to let go. Then you will know a walk to happiness, it's waiting at the end of the line. If you keep going you'll get far. For every scar paints hope. A new vision therefore.

PART II
AGAINST THE CURRENT

"Learn to love without condition. Talk without bad intention. Give without any reason. And most of all, care for people without expectation."

OF THE MEMORY THAT serves your being. It could be hard. Or face them with gratitude and see what's on the other side. When you learn to accept the fact, the easier it becomes. Not as strong as a rock but when it shatters, you'll find freedom. The mind is the closest state of being. Don't tire yourself. If heartache is not what you desire, don't let it be. Pain is everywhere. It travels. It is not permanent. They are part of the pieces. Of nightmares.

In the ground, a growling sound slowly emerged but a voice asking for help.

As if it was buried deep being there for a while. It was a loud noise you can hear the whispers. The murmurs. They were saying something. Like a name. Someone you didn't know. The echoes inside your head. The leap that you must take is part of it. Discover other things. You have to experience them to fully understand. There is a story behind it. In the dusk you'll see a shadow coming toward you. Don't be afraid. Don't let the waves catch you. For trials are overwhelming sometimes. See for yourself in front of your eyes there might be a transformation. You'll see why. Changes in life are inescapable. Day and night are immortalized with conviction.

Of hope and faith.

There is a cure to be found. That is regarded somewhere.

There are many reasons why it hurts. Not only for the truth. But it builds an illusion of despair and betrayal. Those feelings you don't want. You try to avoid them as they come after you. A play of mind and emotions. An insult. You seem to hear them laugh. The echoes inside your head. Thoughts that don't make sense.

Imagine this. Imagining things.

It's been a while since Emilia went to see Dr. Paula. She's her therapist for five years now. She refused to go at first but a requirement for her. It became voluntary when she finally felt comfortable. Dr. Paula is pleasant, that's Emilia's impression. She listens to her very attentively.

She felt her story. She listens.

A true connection. Dr. Paula lost her son eight years ago. She told this to Emilia. In better understanding of what she's going through. And when she said she understood. She meant it.

Emilia had trouble sleeping for the last week.

Her nightmares were coming back again. She was seeing her mother covered with blood in an empty room—faded, unrecognized. She tried to call on her name. Mother. Mother. But the words wouldn't come out. She squeezed her hands tightly and grasp for air to breathe again. She's had all different kinds of nightmares since she was a kid. As if she's gotten used to them. Although she tried to convince herself they were memories of them, she still has trouble in her head. The panic attacks were inconsistent, at least for the last two weeks. Emilia didn't want to forget about them. The only way she can remember. But she didn't want to go on to live with the misery that's riding on her for years. The emptiness that's surging from within. She didn't want to recollect that part. It was too much. With nobody else by her side. She grew up with a dark reality of the past. She figured she might as well just suffer.

A dream she had for a while. It keeps coming back. Of her being on the beach, with her feet on the water. Later on trying to catch the waves, she found herself drowning in the middle. She tried to ask for help. She screamed. But no one was there.

She was slowly sinking when a silhouette of a man came toward her. She couldn't make of who he was. He reached for her hand. She was pulled out. She woke up.

"Do you still think of them?" asked Dr. Paula. "Yes, everyday." said Emilia.

Her parents were killed in an ambush. They weren't supposed to be there. She didn't see it—of what happened. Although her imagination replayed a scenario over and over. Her father had to beg for their lives. Let them go and they would tell no one. But the man decided to pull the trigger. Then left the scene.

She didn't understand at first. She didn't grow with hatred.

All their sympathetic attitudes and questions that didn't mean anything to her.

For an eleven-year-old to have lost everything, she didn't have anywhere to go. When she was adopted by a wealthy family—a couple who didn't have a child. Somehow she was given a new life. They took her as their own. Emilia thought to herself and probably the only thing she was thankful for.

Life is shared with the ones you love. It is the most euphoric feeling in the world. You are given a piece of you. With this find yourself. You see togetherness. And be delighted by it. It was a chance given. A chance by heart. When you make the right choices, you will be rewarded in the end. You must seek the true meaning of existence. Today you strive. Going against the grain. And by that, it counts the most important value. Make sure you are the happiest in everything that you do. It matters. Loneliness is subdued to its innermost part. Emilia took her step day by day. She recognized the pain. She found what was lost. Although it was hard, she needed to experience them all at once. The only way she could've gotten over it. It wasn't over.

Emilia thought about love. She relinquished the hope of finding it in different forms, and from different people. Everything changed when she met Albert. She was alive again. She took notice of the things she didn't pay attention to. She learned about different things for the first time. Like planting and cooking—some of the things they did together. He knew all sorts of things when it comes to plants. Almost everyday he gave her flowers. Not a bouquet but the single stems. He took care of her. Little did she know it wasn't for long. Happiness is to be chased. She thought about it.

"Why do we have the things that we don't need and lose the ones that are important?"

There were so many questions she asked of herself.

She looked up the sky. And screamed.

She yelled at it. She was angry. Emilia felt a burning sentiment inside of her. She cried. She thought about it. If her life was made for sadness. If she was born to suffer. And why. She was losing faith. She didn't want to believe in anything. She's a target. To cover up with great melancholy. It was taunting her. It wasn't a game, but she had to play it. She plays to trick her mind. The only way she could do it. She knew she had to divert herself. In her mind. She designed a life totally different. Perhaps a lie. But in a way to escape misery. She'd rather do it. She didn't want to remember any. She wanted to start again. And let all the waves gush forth toward a different direction. It was the thing she wanted. She was ready. As long as she's fighting for it. One thing. The universe is not against you. You only need to realize, at first, and when you do you'll be able to decide. There's pain and sorrow. That will always be part of it. But once recognized they'll be nothing but fragments floating in the dust. Emilia left Pennsylvania to move somewhere. Where she hopes to find happiness—and maybe she will. But the most important thing is to live with peace of mind. Those things that used to mean to her didn't exist anymore. It was only a thought and remained there for as long as it could.

———

"Someday, everything will make perfect sense. So for now, laugh at the confusion, smile through the tears, and keep reminding yourself that everything happens for a reason."

———

Fall of May, Emilia somewhat had a bleak vision. Of how she would have to live a life of suffering and wonder. The path she didn't choose has already been chosen for her. She refused to take it. But like a wind it travels around, in the end it'll come back. She thought maybe her acceptance will help. Only then she'd be able to cross. It wasn't easy. As if it wasn't for her to understand. If she was oblivious, she was not human. She couldn't be. We go to places. We will never know. There is a force behind of which soon divides your attention. It was an intended trap for those who easily fall for it. It was meant to be like that. It's not supposed to be easy. If it was then everyone would have done it. The reason of why such things are alive. Why they exist. Why do we? For a moment you see a flicker. That's a little light. When you are headed the right way. The wind is not going to be steady. A force that pulls. Sometimes they want you to be mad. They tease you only to see how you'd react. When you learn to glide against the current, you'd soon be able to swim into your own direction. With your own actions, you'll be guided.

Emilia used to frequent at the museum. In fact, she has a favorite piece called "Young Girl with a Goldfish" by Edmond

Francois Aman-Jean. She finds the arts remarkably interesting. While looking at paintings and artworks became one of her pastimes she thought about the difference of dreams and reality. Where she can feel every inch of emotion that comes along. There's no more denying. She must face her fears. And so, all the trembles and tears she must withstand. If they don't mean anything they'll be gone. She should've known that all of this is nothing but one piece of the puzzle. Perhaps an element of a greater picture. Her days maybe gloomy and covered with doubts. She questions herself and all the people around. The mind is temporarily replaced with new memories. Nevertheless, what's inside of you will be a reflection. What she needs to conceal her feelings? But she is vulnerable to the past. She's been carrying it with her for a while. Emilia holds onto it, not to plot a revenge. She is not a sadist to herself. However, the only way to connect with them. It was hard enough to weigh two things. She didn't have anybody to share. As a kid she didn't have an idea of what she'd like to become. For so long she's been used to being a lonely soul. Of which at times she thought about as an escape. It was good at first but eventually became a burden. Her loss and grief. There's no way of putting it. Emilia must find her purpose. For just a little bit she continues to believe.

Although there's no sense of complaining. She only does that in her head. She'll be alright

All that remains now is a memory. That she will cherish. They were once part of her.

Clouds part their ways. She sees the sky very clearly. She breathes. A part of her that wanders. She finds hope to where she goes.

Ignited with the light that she holds. She must create a dream.

"I don't know which step you'd want me to take. I'll do it if that's what it takes. And if that makes you happy. I am tired of sadness and grief. I've lived with them for years."

Emilia opens an old box. Where there she hid a picture of her parents. The faces she memorized. She didn't want to forget them. She is haunted again. It's becoming more and more. Days have passed but nothing's changed. Her thoughts have become bigger and more troubled. Unable to close her eyes, she couldn't sleep. Emilia is taken to an open field. Where she stands in the middle. Looking up the sky, she didn't know where she is.

She touched her face. Something didn't feel quite right. The ghosts from the past maybe gone. Somehow they got tired. The waves have calmed down. They have set aside. Perhaps there's nothing to fear this time. They only feed on your weakness and sorrow. They don't exist in the light. Emotions continue to rise. They couldn't be suppressed. Not for a long time. She must first recognize. Better yet, she must reconcile with it. Emilia thinks that she's been punished with no reason. A bearer of misfortune. To which her parents paid for. And even herself is paying for it. It was hard to find reality in the midst of her trouble and anxiety. Her truth maybe different. She lives to bear both pain and joy. Yes, for a moment she was happy. It didn't take long. The acknowledgment that has been a long time coming. She found a pale white feather. It was sitting right there. By the window. She was a wallflower. But it didn't bother her. Those were the things that don't interest her. Her solitude has given her time to embrace what's in front of her. Abundance of space where she forcefully glides upon. Laying on the floor made of hardwood. She spreads her arms like that of a cross. With a blank face she stares at the ceiling. She thinks.

The story is not the same. It was just a thought. Dr. Paula once told her that in loneliness she'll find herself. There's no other person worth knowing. And when she does maybe and somehow she'll find what she's been looking for. The void she kept. She must be willing to surrender. At the park where she takes photos. She doesn't need them to be perfect. She likes the candid shots. When every object breathes. It gives more meaning to life. After all, when everything is vanished in the sun, it remains inside her heart. A picture of a girl holding her mother's hand.

If in your dreams you can do anything. What would you do? If you jump, then you take a risk. And once in your life you do that one thing you've always wanted to do. It all depends on your intention. You live with the consequences in life. It's simple and complicated at the same time. It's hard to understand from the beginning. Nothing makes sense. The dark clouds will soon be gone. What needs to be done? If you can do it now, do it while you can. Everyday is like counting days. She didn't want to wait. But she's becoming used to it. It was a different feeling for her to wake up in the morning. She didn't have much to do. But she's starting over.

———

It wasn't too long ago, when the sea was calmed enough to carry the sun that sets in the West. That girl, she grew up; but not to prolong this agony a new beginning must come. This is where it all ends.

Articles

Women with Parkinson's Need More Support

Women who are under the age of 50 made approximately 3-5% of women diagnosed with Parkinson's disease.

Although there is no cure, medications and support can help. In a recent study at the University of Pennsylvania School of Medicine, there is a disadvantage for those women who don't have caregivers.

"Care provided by family and friends to people with Parkinson's disease is an important source of support, and our findings show that women living with Parkinson's are less likely to receive this support than men," said Dr. Nabila Dahodwala, an associate professor of neurology.

The study covered 7,209 patients at 21 centers in the United States, Canada, the Netherlands and Israel. The results were also based on prior observations and reports that 79 percent of female patients have a caregiver compared to 88 percent for male patients.

While there were no specific reasons for the disparity of male and female caregiver support, it raised questions and highlights the general need for more support of elderly women with disabilities.

Vaping, an Alternative to Smoking

More and more teenagers are using vaping than regular cigarettes. Although there is a relative impact to it as opposed to smoking, an alternative that could entice the younger generation.

According to Center for Disease Control and Prevention with its current statistics, 5.6 million of today's Americans younger than 18 will die early from a smoking-related illness.

In 2016, about 2 of every 100 middle school students (2.2%) reportedly used smokeless tobacco. The use of multiple tobacco products is prevalent among youth. Research study also showed more US high-school seniors have tried vaping compared to traditional smoking.

The nicotine component is not only addictive but life-threatening. Cigarette smoking is still the number one risk factor for lung cancer. Tobacco is a toxic mix of more than 7,000 chemicals.

There are many reasons why teenage smoking has increased—one of them is peer pressure. Social factor plays a significant role in terms of the decision making for the young generation. Partly, most of them wanted to fit in certain cliques or to impress other social groups.

Without the proper guidance from their parents or adults there will be consequences in their co-mingling.

Municipalities in Chicago area and across the county are taking steps in discouraging teen smoking. With the minimum age hiked last year, from 18 to 21, consumers are forced to follow on the new implementation. It is bad for business but a way to filter the young generation smokers.

It's Time to Get Serious about Climate Change

When former Vice President Al Gore released his documentary in 2006 entitled "An Inconvenient Truth" somehow the public was lectured with the consequences of global warming. Some may have missed it. But truth of the matter—climate change is real.

More than before it has become more obvious. The natural calamities last year were undeniable. Hurricane Harvey which inflicted the Houston metropolitan area costing nearly $200 billion, while Hurricane Maria destroyed Puerto Rico making it the strongest storm to make a landfall in 85 years.

Whether or not a testament to the ever changing weather condition not only in the United States but all over the world, those events could be an eye-opener for us and the government to do something.

The Federal Emergency Management Agency (FEMA) which was created in 1979, is one of the aiding organizations to provide assistance for disaster relief depending on which the funds are necessary under the law and declaration process.

Once the governor has requested help and the President has approved, this will eventually be declared as major disaster. However, as mentioned, this all goes in a process. But the wait cannot sustain the families and individuals who have been affected by the disaster.

Typhoons and hurricanes that could damage a large part of the community are expected to have cost millions of dollars in devastation. Although local and emergency funds maybe requested, they don't come fast or easy. The people who have already lost their homes will have to endure a long wait to get assistance. The immediate need for food and medicine are top priorities.

Some agencies may also provide grants for home repairs and low interest loans for small business relief. No matter what the preparations—these types of calamities cannot be stopped, even so, there should be enough resources to cover the relief programs from the government. Otherwise donations and assistance from other non-profit organizations are very much needed.

Climate Change has showed its severe impact in large scale destruction to mankind and the environment we are living in. The unrolling cold weather that continues to blanket the eastern U.S. can be an example of the biggest changes that we have to expect entering this new year.

Many experts are also blaming this cold season on climate change—at least it is part of the problem.

The linking of the weather patterns which left unusual outcomes noticeably in southern region with the experience of icy winter and low temperature. On the other hand, Thomas Fire is considered the largest wildfire to ignite Southern California with significant widespread of property loses scorching nearly 282,000 acres.

Last year a huge crack in one of Antarctica's largest ice shelves had scientists shaking their coats and still closely monitoring before it makes another rift.

Perhaps it's about time to get serious and pay more attention to the environmental needs that we are facing today. This could be a challenge but to preserve our own habitat from the dangers that circulate around it—a vital aspect of our existence. We have but one world. We need to protect it.

Success is a Mindset

Nobody said it was going to be easy. The road to success that is. And yet, people tend to forget the sensibility of being successful. A lot of these motivational talks and videos that we see very often are products of other people's desires and goals.

The realization being that without hard work and perseverance there can only be failure. It was not to discourage the lowest but for most of us, who don't dwell on listening to a five-minute inspirational audio clip we do what we can do best everyday.

The essence really of being successful is only in your mind. Once you've realized the things that you want to accomplish in life and take steps to move forward that is the beginning of the process. Because everything that comes along in life can be a learning point. The journey towards your goal is an impeccable attribution to what you want to become.

"Success is the progressive realization of a worthy goal or ideal," according to Earl Nightingale. Wherein people should start giving value to the simplest things in life that are part of a transformation. While the focus is to become successful let us not forget the meaning of success. What it means to be successful in the first place? Is it the money? The fame? The title? None of these things can truly justify the value of success because they diminish.

On the other hand, when you have established something for yourself as well as with other people with the sense of longevity you are giving more to what is being expected. When you embrace the process of being successful in whichever area you are trying to pursue you are already giving yourself an edge against the competition. By then you are opening your mind to a more completely complicated but rather authentic form of success in life. And when that happens another form shall take place which is also known as happiness. Again, that's another aspect.

Making a Living, New Orleans

NEW ORLEANS, LOUISIANA—A man pushing platform cart with boxes to deliver. Roadway and sidewalks reconstruction undergone on Bourbon Street from St. Louis to Dumaine streets on September 17, 2018. As part of the Infrastructure Improvement Project the City of New Orleans, Department of Public Works, Sewerage & Water Board partnered together to improve the historical streets and corners of the French Quarter. Meanwhile, artists are now free to sell their works anywhere in the French Quarter even without permit following the decision of Louisiana Supreme Court voting 5–2 to strike down New Orleans' ban on outdoor art sales with no permit.

Only 200 A permits are granted a year making it more difficult to obtain for artists who are interested to sell their works particularly on the streets of Jackson Square. Although many street performers and artists are visible throughout the area, the city has been trying to regulate those who participate in such sales activities.

New Campaign Raised Awareness on Kids and Social Media

With the hype of technology and social media everything seems to be a click away from getting that information of which some are not suitable for the young children. Many parents are concerned with the continues rise of online media and the interest that's capturing the minds of the young generation.

From Facebook to Instagram and YouTube, every single person seems to be online clicking from one video to another. At least that's a fact. Everyone now is connected to social media whether for personal or business use.

With that comes a group of people who will try to limit and change the possibilities of the future. Hopefully. Truth About Tech is a campaign launched by the Center for Humane Technology in partnership with nonprofit Common Sense.

This is an attempt to raise awareness not only to the public but also to tech companies to create more user-friendly content in the digital age. With the rising percentage of kids and adults being addicted to gadgets and internet there is a need to implement non-intrusive and less addictive products.

STRANGERS PHOTO SERIES Q & A

A background of this collection.

How did you pick the location?

That was such a random trip and for some reason I decided to wander around the French Quarter. They had some major road repairs going on that time. I think New Orleans is such a vibrant city and you can see that art plays a huge role in their culture, so to know that there was a ban I could only sympathize. The "Big Easy" is not complete without their street performers, musicians, and artists.

What is your style and inspiration?

When I started taking pictures that day my goal was to create a hyperlapse (featured on *Drums*) and that was it. But I kind of went the other way. At first, I called it "*Strangers on Vacation*" because of all the different people coming from different places. Although if you've been to New Orleans you know it's special down there. It's like southern hospitality with a flair of European accent. I decided to go black and white on this one as an ode to irony. The loud colors you see from every corner of Bourbon Street were silent in the photos.

Tell us about the essay collection.

Well, this one is long overdue. I have been writing for years and I finally took the liberty of sharing some of them in order to express myself. There are so much complexity happening in our world today, but I think it's good to take a pause at times needed. This book is more of a collection of thoughts that I've had for a long time. Some of them are deeply personal and I hope that it would somehow shed some light to the significant issues we are all experiencing these days.

What are your thoughts about the Dark Tides?

Having been able to work in both corporate and publishing industries taught me a lot. In a way, I discovered so many things and learned to apply them in every given situation. I think that we should acknowledge our distinct experiences because they serve as steppingstones to where exactly we want to go. I would like to advise the young generation to reflect of the things that matter most to them, and not be caught up with the noise in the society. If you are good at something try to pursue it no matter what. One thing that surprised me during this whole process is that, there's an opportunity to almost everything. You have to consider looking at a different perspective and see more clearly, to create a vision. But while it can be confusing sometimes remember to look around and see yourself apart from the rest.

EPILOGUE

In modern age people are accustomed to shared information, although privacy policies are somewhat undermined with the prevalence of cyberbullying particularly in social media. The use of hate comments and bias language are becoming subversive in such a way that provokes unwanted interaction between readers or the public. Without the intention of participating in an ongoing debate and whether or not you realized that you should have kept your opinion to yourself, sometimes it can be a little too late. An unseen force, that is, the power of words. One can inspire, others will deny. Thus, psycholinguistic implications need further examining in cases of diverse audience both sympathetic and not to a topic. Not only the subject but the tone of writing has great potential of emotional contagion. *"The essence really of being successful is only in your mind,"* is a line in an article I wrote about self-awareness. For the most part it gained a lot of positive comments especially to those who seek motivational quotes to start off their day. It was a good feeling to have that kind of response. Interestingly, an opposite turnout for a different article I wrote which talked about the rising problem of vaping. To me, it was a question of content. Were the readers unfavorable of the topic? I supposed it was not what I expected. As an educator with background in creative writing, arts, and communication, I work on understanding human cognitive abilities and in relation to behavioral variation, both oral and written. It was out of interest and willingness to better understand such influence that I see an opportunity for pertinent research in this field. Perhaps in social context a reader's comment or feedback of a book is merely a reaction to its content. There are more responsible users on social media that tend to follow-up on their comments, including justification of the language, and again, we go back to our differences in beliefs, characteristics and expectations. I am interested in finding out the biases in relation to literature and psycholinguistic influence. Although my experience in print media has taught me a lot with fact checking for the purpose of investigative reporting—it was also a realization to determine of "what sells" to the public. In theory, my tendency of adjusting the subject in writing was based on the criteria of trend and suggestion rather than inspiration. The published work entitled "*The Hummingbird*" is more of a compilation in that sense. I would like to examine the biases in topics and language with its different contents. After finishing my master's degree, I had the opportunity to work in the public school system where I witnessed the disparity of interests between young students in K-12. While some tried to conform in the old teaching commons, others were more excited to dive into real-world learning. Millennials are more risk takers, adventurous and spontaneous which proves to show that textbook reading will not be sufficed to educate them. One of the effects of social media is interconnection—the ability of people's mind to relate to current events. So many of the topics curated now are made for certain groups of people, demographics or target audience. A question of whether society is influencing literature or the other way around.

A compilation of stories, essays and news articles that I have written over the past few years will be examined in part of the research process, and in observation to the proposal. It would be a tremendous opportunity for me to be able to pursue this study. At the same time, I have full confidence in the relevant faculty that would serve as the examiner for this evaluation. I imagine that the university has extensive resources in respective subject areas that would be useful to all students. While my circumstances slightly require a careful deliberation in consideration, it would mean an utmost significance to be able to explore and contribute the end results of this research.

REFERENCES

Borden, Gloria J. et al (1994) Speech Science Primer, Lippincott Williams and Wilkins 351 West Camden St., Baltimore MD 21201-2436 USA

Dodge, Ellen P. (2000) The Survival Guide for School based Speech-Language Pathologist, Delmar. Thompson Learning, 401 West "A" Sheet, Suit 325 San Diego, CA, USA

Gerber, Adele (1993) Language Related Learning Disabilities, Paul H. Brooks Publishing Co., Inc. P.O. Box 10624, Baltimore, Maryland, 21285-0624

Kuder, S. Jay, (2003) Teaching Students with Language and Communication Disabilities, Allyn and Beacon, Inc 75 Arlington St., Boston MA 02116

Ling, Daniel (1989) Foundation of Spoken Language for Hearing Impaired Children, AG Bell 3417 Volta Place, NW, Washington DC 2007, USA

Owens, Robert E et al (2003) An Introduction to Communication Disorders, Allyn and Bacon Inc., 75 Arlington St., Boston MA 02116

Paul, Rhea (2002) Introduction to Clinical Methods in Communication Disorders, Paul H. Brooks, Publishing Co, Inc., P.O. Box 10624 Baltimore Maryland 21285-0624

Siegel, Bryna (2003) Helping Children With Autism Learn, Oxford University Press, 198 Makison Ave., NY New York 10016

Smith, Ann Bosma (2004) Articulation and Phonology, Resource Guide for School Age Children and Adults. Thompson Delmar Learning, 5 Maxwell Drive, Clifton Park NY 12065

Sousa, Daniel A. (2001) How the Special Needs Brains Learn, Corwin Press, Inc., 2455, Teloler Road, Thousand Oaks, CA 91320

Hall, B.J., Oyer, H.J., & Haas, W.H (2001). Speech, language and hearing disorders. A guide for the teacher (3rd ed). Boston, MA : Allyn & Bacon.

For inquiries on bulk orders, discounts, and other opportunities, you can connect with us through social media and our website.

A preview of

Gathering

A Poetry Collection

Author of "IN TIME AND WITH WATER"
KATHLEENE QUINN

The Throne

What will take you to the other side
wherein thoughts are for free
although freedom costs
convince me with every word you speak
they called from Oxford, suited, fitted
only on the surface—these groups come differently
they mingle in so called generations
collision—*a chemical reaction*
but too much to show and pretend
they are the greatest
we have plenty of choices in the midst of
worries and campaign
the stadium is calling; they dress up
like hypocrites
experts of the material
don't know what they're made of—
who deserves the throne?
not an empire of your own
a world built for people   those who believe
and fight
show them your cards.

Exist

Beneath the ground something growls
dry piece of soil, cracked, useless dusty wind
filled the atmosphere
a leaf no longer green
gasping for oxygen
a survival of existence   absence of daylight
pour no rain
in no time an open field sprout no seeds,
no plant roots crawling down under
foggy, withered, unwanted the dark side of the sun,
a storm just for once   amuse us

with the growth stems like veins, trapped in the corner
                                        cut them
hundred days later and one will turn
into flower not sour nor bitter
the long wait is over, let them drink up.

Garden

Gloomy days never seem to end without a light
and even in darkness a single breath of hope is impossible
no one seems to hear a whisper
a scream—of a little girl lost in the garden,
a poison Ivy thorns from the past linger
not so green leaves surrounding
sadden by a fact of lies and chances
not given as always
when did you see yourself in the mirror?

An Oath

Meaningless without even understanding
the truth behind it
look further, but never forget to look behind
things are hidden in the nearest place
Apollo is not so distant; use as a weapon,
a challenge to simplicity, a satellite in disguise, rotation—
rotating counter clockwise
in western civilization Emancipation, an attempt;
a mistake
no more participation of rallies and parade
"for such a long time we fight for what is right, but are we
already tired, being played and fooled around like puppets, and
for what purpose supposedly an oath to Liberty."

No counting

Those tears cannot be counted meters by far you go
don't surrender it won't grow
not moving from where you are
but distance doesn't matter with every encounter no counting
          keep dancing, to life there's never ending

Rally

Pity the pure hearted—
the young and innocent whose story is yet to be heard,
unknowingly murdered with judgement like dead leaves
blown by the wind further and more

echoes traveled from past to present
nothing but scattered memories
the unknown, unfamiliar faces
where they build columns and bridges

A city where people walk around in fear and doubt
they sing an old song   *hum—humming*
no empty corner
not a single post or canal   is alone everybody
is staring, broken, unfitting—
if only faith was sewn into their sleeves
unintended trust but asking for forgiveness
she cries, she cries
unhappily walking down the streets of Broadway
embracing the odds of loneliness it fell
from the inside again with angry voices
they appear suddenly in the rally

If you see where I am standing
does it pain you then
when I don't belong to anyone

there's a voice coming from the sand
with nothing but a fragile heart
do you remember where it all began?
If you can see where I am going
will you come with me
there are no boundaries only reality
of truth and lies
look beyond what you see   there somehow you will find
me

Whistle

Whistle in the wind soleness of the night
—absence of words *better than* your lies
thoughts running in streams   a nightmare not a dream
cold breeze but burning eyes

touch thy skin a little   a sudden change no regrets,
display no forgiveness   there's no hate without love
like day and night departed by fate
not a choice of heart   one could only hear like a secret
you tell again whistle in the wind

Fallen Angel

The face of a fallen angel have you seen it?
You might
          but didn't notice
thunder and lightning strike abode
of the darkness   refuge of loneliness
there's a space between those two holes
a burning grass
you're tired   she cried
          a guardian angel hand in hand
open skies   say goodbye   an angel in disguise

Strokes and Lines

Charcoal maybe dark in color
the shades remind you of the past
they tell your story of which
in every stroke the lines are connected
    tell them what they don't know
a surprise, a gesture,   a thought that's buried
deep inside
look around in the wildest forest
twigs and branches shake hands
drink the water   from the river
you'll come back

Camouflage

How do you care so much about nothing?
You question what you haven't seen
letting the pessimist enter your head
give a little stare to every move
they're trying at least;
not to make the same mistake again
trust is not given by hand
it has to be earned
tell a secret for whom to keep
don't tire yourself in wondering what has been
go with the flow and be a camouflage
like a chameleon,
a season   people change habits
—a State of Mind
pretending wisely with the master
show less of everything
surprise reality with treachery.